W9-AHT-000

The
Mike King
Story

The
Mike King
Story

Mike King

Good Books®

Intercourse, PA 17534

Photograph Credits

Many of the early photos in this book were provided by Mike King and his family members. The rest of the photos were taken by Lauren Martin, Lisa Wagner, and Mike King (with the help of their friends), except the following: Kenneth Pellman, 20 (top), 168; Greg Petersheim, 41; Jacob Wiebe, 42; Eileen Tymon, 44 and 45; *Intelligencer Journal*/Barry Zercher, 46; Jonathon Charles, 48; Myron Stoltzfus, 58 (top); *Festival Quarterly*/Craig Heisey, 61; John Vastyan, 63; Associated Press/Paul Vathis, 64; *Colorado Springs Sun*/Mark Reis, 94 and 95; Associated Press/Brett Johnson, 123; *The Elizabethtown Chronicle*, 137; *Intelligencer Journal*/Dan Marschka, 138; Patriot News Co./Norman Arnold, 139; *Lebanon Daily News*/Howard Kolus, 140 and 141; *Chester County Press*/Jim Dugan, 146 and 147; Jim Graham, 161.

The illustration on page 42 is reprinted with permission from *Spinal Cord Injuries*, edited by Roberta B. Trieschmann, 1980, Pergamon Press, Inc.

Design by Craig Heisey.

THE MIKE KING STORY
Copyright © 1985 by Mike King
International Standard Book Number: 0-934672-33-4
Library of Congress Catalog Card Number: 85-81940

All rights reserved. Printed in the United States of America. No part of this book may be reproduced in any manner, except for brief quotations in critical articles or reviews, without permission.

Published by Good Books, Intercourse, PA 17534

Dedication

To all those people for whom I made
my wheelchair trip—
the handicapped and disabled
everywhere.

May you have courage and determination
to reach for your goals and dreams.

A portion of the royalties from
this book
will go to handicap
organizations,
furthering the benefits
of their programs.

Table of Contents

Challenge of a Lifetime   11
The Accident   14
     Album One: Growing Up   17
The Hospital   25
The Flight Home   28
Dad and Mom, My Four Brothers, and Me   31
Fixing My Back   35
No Call Buttons   38
     Album Two: Accident and Recovery   41
How My Family Took It all   51
Deciding to Live   54
     Album Three: College and Travel   57

College, Too   67
Getting Along Without Working Legs   71
Album Four: Alaska and the Yukon   73
Planning the Trip   85
Album Five: Calgary to Colorado   89
The Road Team and How They Made It Work   98
On the Road   101
Album Six: Wichita to Kansas City   105
Chills, Hills, Gravel, and Rain   115
Mixing Up the Monotony   119
Album Seven: Ozarks to Appalachians   121
If We Were Doing It Again   136
Album Eight: Home to Pennsylvania   137
I Learned A Lot   155
Everything You Ever Wanted to Know About
Wheelchairs   158
Album Nine: The Final Stretch   161
The Rest of My Life   169
A Word to Able-bodied People   172
We're All Handicapped   174

Acknowledgements

My deepest thanks to all who helped make my wheelchair
trip possible—

- The Hope for Life board who organized and arranged the trip's
financing—J. Myron Stoltzfus, Isaac H. Stoltzfus, Eileen M.
Tymon, John S. Stoltzfus, Francis I. duPont, Herman Glick, Dr.
Edwards P. Schwentker, R. Douglas Good, and Allon H.
Lefever.

- Norm Kurtz of Twin Pine Auto Sales who supplied our van;
Horning Dodge who loaned another road-team vehicle; and
Herman Glick who let us use one of his cars.

- Messiah College, who provided five students to promote the
trip and help carry it off.

- The road team itself—Curt King, James Graybill, Tim Raber, Lauren Martin, Glenn Stoltzfus, and the Messiah students— Tim Haines, Steve Engle, Terri Shimer, Lisa Wagner, and Diane Broujos.

- All the people along the way who gave support—especially those who planned publicity and fundraising events, the rehab centers and hospitals who opened their doors to us, the Mennonite Church and Mennonite Central Committee who helped us make contacts nationally.

- The two restaurants who hosted fundraisers in Lancaster County—Good 'n Plenty Restaurant for the pre-trip banquet and Dutch Town and Country Inn for the post-trip banquet.

- My family, who has been with me in all my efforts and struggles—Mom, for her endless encouragement and support; Dad, for giving me determination to make the best of whatever comes; Rod, Curt, Kent, and Wendel, my brothers, who keep me from stepping out of line, but more than that, give me the confidence to do whatever I am capable of.

Challenge of a Lifetime

I had a raw blister on each hand, right where I hit the push rail. My cold was getting worse. James pointed out that I hadn't smiled in days. And it was only Thursday. I had left Fairbanks on Tuesday, three days earlier. But all my training, all the well-wishers back home, all my guts and confidence weren't going to get me over the mountains, let alone through the rugged surface that passes for paving on the Alaskan Highway.

I wheeled a hundred yards, turned my chair sideways toward the shoulder to rest, and tried to figure out how to get out of this trip. The more breaks I took, the more I wanted.

My brother Curt and our cousin James kept jumping out of the van they were supposed to be driving behind me and tried to talk me back into wheeling.

"Should we push you?" they asked. "What should we do?"

"No, you can't push me!" I yelled. "I'm supposed to wheel the distance myself, not get pushed!"

I knew I wasn't abusing myself. I was just physically frustrated because I wasn't in as good shape as I thought I was. Things had to get better fast or I wouldn't even make it into Canada. Forget going to Washington, D.C. The hills, the road surface, and my pitiful endurance were blowing my schedule.

Somehow I got through the day. And after some quarrelling with Curt the next morning about how I wanted my hands taped, I was ready to try again, for awhile.

I expected Curt to have a photographic memory! He'd be taping me up and I'd tell him, "No, not that way!" I had shown him how I wanted it done and he was supposed to remember. I yelled at him; he yelled back. It was good for both of us since we had learned a long time ago how not to hold things against each other.

That day felt a little less like a failure. My body and mind were getting over the shock; my blisters were healing enough that the pain didn't slow me down anymore; I was starting to adjust to the routine. An hour north of Delta Junction, Alaska, where we were planning to stop for supper and the night, a car coming from Fairbanks passed us. Then it turned and came back toward us, swung around even with the van that Curt and James were driving and asked what was up. The guys stopped; I kept going. I had miles to make up.

It turned out to be people from the little town—Mrs. Rohr and her daughter, Kim, who was president of the high school senior class and a first-rate planner! When they got back to town the two of them contacted the mayor who arranged free lodging and a free evening meal for us that night.

The next morning we drove back the eight miles to the point where I had stopped the evening before, so I could begin the day. When I came around a turn about five miles out of town, I had another surprise. All forty juniors and seniors from Delta Junction High School were waiting for me on their bikes. They had agreed to bag school that day, without telling their teachers! They were excited about what I was doing and when I pulled up to them, asked if they could ride with me for the day.

"Sure," I said. "Great!" James said I even smiled!

Kim had stopped by our hotel the evening before and checked with Curt about her idea. And the kids had briefed their parents, who had alerted the teachers, so I felt like all three hundred inhabitants of Delta Junction were cheering for me! The guy who ran the Tastee Freeze in town treated the whole pack of us to lunch, and then the kids went on out of town with me for about forty miles. The parents showed up in trucks at the end of the day to haul the kids and bikes back. And we kept going.

Those believing kids couldn't have had better timing. Their energy, their wanting to know more, and their wanting to be part of it turned me around.

The next day I knew I was going to go the whole distance. I wasn't sure I would be on schedule. But I would finish the trip, even if it took a month longer than I had planned. The pain and the terrain weren't going to beat me anymore.

The Accident

Ours was a dream cycle trip. I was twenty years old the summer of 1978 when Greg Petersheim, Merv Stoltzfus, Ron Stoltzfus, and I headed to the West Coast by way of Canada. After reaching the Pacific we were going to come down the coast, and then go back home through the northwestern states.

We were in Banff National Park in Alberta when I failed to see a parked car that was preparing to pull onto the road. I ran into the back end of it, broke my back, both my legs, and suffered a lot of internal injuries as well. And the accident left me with a severed spinal cord so that I was paralyzed from the waist down.

The day was kind of cloudy and rainy. And even though it was August 13, the air was chilly in the low 40's and upper 30's. I remember we had showers off and on.

Between four and five in the afternoon I was just outside the city of Banff on the twenty-mile stretch up to Lake Louise where we were all going to meet later that evening. We were all on our own, taking our time and doing what we wanted to on the way up there.

Greg and Merv were ahead of me and Ron was behind me. I stopped to take pictures of some mule deer along the road. I remember starting off, but that's the last thing I recall except what people have told me since then.

Ron came up on the accident right after it happened. Greg and Merv had stopped to wait for us, and when they saw traffic backing up decided to come back and see where we were.

But I remember nothing from about four o'clock Sunday afternoon until five o'clock Monday evening. Although I was conscious and talking, even answering questions, it seems my mind has simply blocked out the tragedy so it isn't there to haunt me the rest of my life.

Fortunately I had my helmet on when I wrecked, so I had no head injuries. I probably wouldn't be alive if I hadn't been wearing it, at least from the looks of the thing. It was banged up pretty badly. There were times on the trip, when we passed through states that didn't require helmets, that I hadn't worn it.

It turned out that another accident happened near mine at about the same time, so the ambulance from the medical center in Banff was at that site. There was a paramedic, caught in the traffic jam caused by my accident, who had just completed a canoe trip on the river. When he saw my legs were broken he tied canoe oars on them as splints. In fact, he took care of me until a police paddy wagon came to take me to the Banff Medical Center.

When I got there, the staff realized they had more than they could handle so they immediately sent me off to the Foothills Hospital in Calgary. That was an eighty-mile drive, but they freed an ambulance to go and a medical team rode along with me.

I spent most of Sunday night in the operating room, then, while they patched up my internal injuries and worked on fixing the broken femurs in both my legs.

I realized on that trip how often other drivers fail to see approaching motorcycles or misjudge their speed. I would drive toward an intersection and notice a car stopping, starting, and at the last minute, stopping suddenly again because they had only then seen me. So I knew I was vulnerable, but this accident happened so quickly that I didn't have a chance to respond. The police report estimated my speed at forty-five to fifty miles an hour. Whether or not I applied any brakes I'm not sure. Technically the collision was my fault because I ran into the back end of the car.

From the beginning, people who didn't even know me showed a lot of concern for my welfare. While I was in the Foothills Hospital, the paramedic who had helped at the scene of the accident came to see me, although I wasn't conscious at the time. Later he sent me a card, introducing himself and wishing me the best. He was upset because I was in pretty bad shape and the doctors weren't sure I was going to make it. Then at Christmas he wrote to me, and again the following Christmas. I responded to him, but I've never seen him or talked to him.

I did think I might meet him this summer when I wheeled through Calgary. We had good media coverage so I wonder if he may have come to see me, but if he did, I never found out. I am glad he showed such concern for me.

What I did struggle with, beginning in those early weeks, was a terribly depressed feeling that I can recall clearly. I was frustrated, I was angry. I would get mad quickly and easily at anyone who came in and said, "Everything's going to be all right." I'd say to myself, "Yeah, right, what do you know about it?"

In the evenings after people who had come to visit would go home, I'd lay there by myself and try to figure out what life was going to be like. Whether it was worth living when I couldn't walk again. I had no idea what was going to happen.

Album One: Growing Up

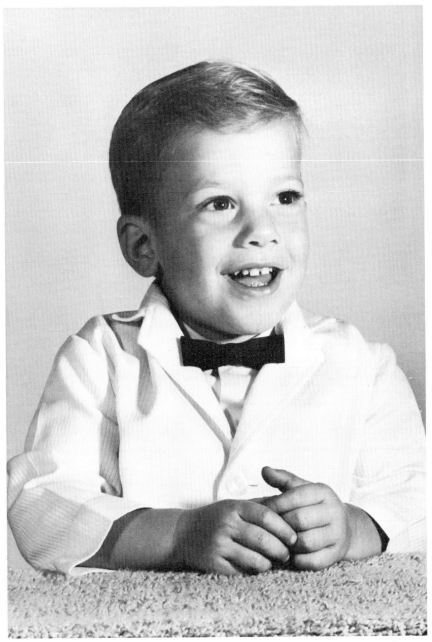

This is a baby picture of me when I was one. We had to wear bow ties in those days.

Here's a typical evening at home with Dad and my brother Rod. As we grew up, Dad often played ball with us after the chores. I suppose that's why we always had an interest in sports.

Below is a family picture taken in January of 1978. Standing in the back row, from left, are Kent, Curt, me and Rod. Front row: Wendel, Mom (Dorothy) and Dad (Paul).

That's me, acting brave, on my first day of school. Actually, I enjoyed school as it turned out.

Growing up on the farm, we always had lots of pets.

Above is my home church, Maple Grove Mennonite.

Grandpa Zook wanted to make sure we had Farmalls instead of John Deeres (he worked for International dealer Bud Hoober).

Upper right is a picture of my home, twenty-five years later (summer of '85). I started helping Dad with the chores on our dairy farm at age seven, but sometimes I got in his way more than I helped him.

I found out that cross-country was my best sport in high school. I'm proud to say our team was undefeated that year. This photo was taken at the fall tournament weekend at Lancaster Mennonite High when I set the new school record.

I graduated from high school in June, 1976.

The Hospital

I didn't know I was in a hospital until Monday afternoon, the day after my accident. I figured that out when I discovered all the tubes in my nose and chest as I woke up to see my parents walking into the room. I knew I must have had an accident but I didn't want to ask any questions.

We were all kind of upset when Mom and Dad got there because they had just learned about my spinal cord injury. And since I was in intensive care, they could only be with me for short bits of time.

Ron and Merv and Greg were at the hospital too. In fact, they stayed around for about a week before Greg and Merv flew home and Ron rode his cycle back to Minnesota. (The other two cycles and mine came back later on a friend's truck.) It seemed none of the guys had any enthusiasm to continue the cycle trip.

It was sometime Tuesday that I asked Mom why I couldn't move my legs. The doctors had told my folks not to tell me more than I asked, so she said that I had hurt my back. I knew about accidents like that, without understanding all the medical details, but at that point I didn't want to hear anymore about it. It was my way of dealing with the possibility that I might not walk again. I wanted to believe I could and would. I refused to think otherwise. That was the end of my questions. I just kind of took each day as it came.

For a week I stayed in intensive care in a room with four other beds, with the drapes kept closed most of the time. They had performed surgery to repair my internal injuries Sunday night, and when they were able to remove the chest tubes and the oxygen tubes from my nose, I was changed to a room on the ninth floor on the mountain side of the hospital. I faced the west and if I turned my eyes far enough I could see the mountains in the distance.

My first roommate was a man from Salt Lake City, whose vacation also ended in the hospital. He learned about Mennonites from us, while we learned about Mormons from him!

When he left, a fortyish-year-old man came in with a spinal cord injury that had happened at work. He was getting ready for surgery the day I was leaving to go back to Pennsylvania. I wished I could know how he managed since I was facing that, too. But my back operation was to be done closer home so I could be near my family while I went through the rehabilitation that would follow it.

All those thoughts were still sort of below the surface for me since I was sure I would walk again. I mean, this kind of thing just couldn't happen to me. I didn't talk about it, I didn't want to hear about it, and the doctors weren't as concerned about that part of my body since their work had been with my broken legs and internal injuries.

Mom and Dad stayed with Jacob and Elsie Wiebe the whole three weeks they were there with me. When the people at the hospital learned we were Mennonites, they gave us Jacob's number. He is the pastor of First Mennonite Church in Calgary. My three friends were hosted by the Leon Penner family from the Foothills Mennonite Church. It was a wonderful connection to have. We all felt such help and support.

When I recovered enough to travel we mapped out the plans to get me back to the Hershey Medical Center in southeastern Pennsylvania. There, an hour and a half from home, I would have my back surgery.

Seldom is it necessary to do an emergency operation for a back injury. Discovering the extent of a spinal cord problem, and then determining the best treatment for it, can be kind of long and tedious. I hadn't suffered any harm by having surgery delayed. It wasn't threatening my life, and no more damage was happening. But now it was time.

And I would soon face a truth I had hoped to avoid. I was paralyzed from the waist down and probably would not walk again.

The Flight Home

There was an airline strike in Canada during the last days of August so we had to figure out another way to get me home.

Wendell Umble, a good friend of ours, was a pilot who, as a teenager, had gone to Canada to do a term of Voluntary Service. He liked it so much he stayed and developed an air service business, flying supplies into the bush. A school friend of Dad's, Fred Gingerich, became his partner. The two of them came down to Foothills to visit us and offered to help if we needed them. It was a great solution for getting out of the country!

They folded the seats down on one side of their twin engine plane and laid me in on a stretcher. I wasn't able to sit up because my back was still broken. But we all fit in—Mom and Dad, me, and Dr. Dystra from the Foothills Hospital who went with us the whole way to Harrisburg.

A friend of Wendell's flew us into Great Falls, Montana. An ambulance crew met us there to move me from the little municipal airport to the international airport where we were to get a Northwest Orient flight into Chicago.

We had to buy six seats since I needed three of them! And we needed to be in first class because of the extra room there. Once again, the crew folded down the seats and fastened my stretcher and me down on top of them.

At first the airline was jumpy about carrying me because they didn't want the responsibility if something happened to me while flying. They were also concerned that the whole thing might bother the other passengers. But they finally did agree to have us, and the flight attendants were as courteous and helpful as they could be. They checked constantly to see if we needed anything.

We had a two-hour layover in Chicago. Another ambulance team met us and helped us get to the TWA waiting room. The only way into it was by elevator, but my stretcher wouldn't fit in there flat, so they tilted me at about a thirty degree angle. After having been on my back three weeks, I would get lightheaded if my head was higher than my feet. I nearly fainted till we got to the second floor because it was the first time my head had been substantially raised since the accident! The crew waited with us then until it was time to board the plane.

The weather was beautiful. We were treated royally. In fact, for about a year after that, Jamie Thompson, the head stewardess, would send me postcards from the different places she flew to. Every time I fly TWA I wonder if I might see her again.

Dr. Ned Schwentker, who would do my surgery at Hershey Medical Center, and Eileen Tymon, who would oversee my rehab program at the Elizabethtown Hospital, stood on the runway at the Harrisburg Airport as we arrived, so they could immediately assess my condition and assist in removing me from the airplane.

When they wheeled me into the airport, all four of my brothers were waiting. Even Rodney, my older brother, had come from Goshen, Indiana, where he was in college. When we saw each other, none of us could say a thing. We all just broke down and cried. Finally, I said, "Hey guys, don't cry. I'm home. I'm home. I'm home."

It was about eight o'clock in the evening when they put me in my room at Hershey. It was a long day. We had left Calgary at nine that morning.

Dad and Mom, My Four Brothers, and Me

My family and my church were the two most important forces in my life when I was a kid. Our fun and our work centered there.

Dad and Mom had five boys, no girls, and a dairy farm! Rodney is a year and a half older than I am; I'm second, born July 29, 1958; Curt is four years younger than I am; Kent follows him by two years; and Wendel comes last, seven years later.

We always had plenty to do. In the early years our farming operation was somewhat smaller, but we presently milk seventy-eight cows and have a total of about one hundred thirty head of cattle. Dad and Mom own two hundred acres of land of which one hundred fifty are tillable, and they rent another hundred-acre farm. Our home place is in Chester County, Pennsylvania, in the southeast corner of the state.

There are five of us guys, and when we weren't on duty in the barn or in the fields, we were playing some kind of ball. And we had a pretty lively, competitive spirit among us. We were always trying to outdo each other, not in a mean sort of way, but to help each other achieve and excel in sports.

Dad liked baseball and played on a church team and he used to play with us a lot after supper in the summertime. When I was in fourth grade he got hit on the back of the head with a bat at home plate. The batter swung around in a complete circle and Dad got caught. He was unconscious for several days and had to have surgery to release pressure in his head. I was too young to realize how seriously he was hurt, but I do remember that Mom was concerned and that a lot of our relatives came to help with the work.

Dad recovered, and I gave no real thought to what a permanent disability, or even dying, would be like.

I had some minor scrapes, and so did my brothers. I first broke a bone—my collarbone—when I was three. When I was five I fell out of a tree and broke my collarbone again. Then when I was ten I tried to beat a cow out of the barn and my arm got pinched—and broken—in the doorway. During my junior year of high school I broke my elbow riding dirt bike and a year later I broke it again playing ice hockey.

I guess every family in a close community gains a certain reputation! And we earned ours. People saw us as a physical, go-get-'em bunch because we were usually moving fast or starting something. I've also heard people say, "You've got to understand, he's a King!" That seems to be a reference to another quality we all share, in varying degrees of course: determination and sheer strongheadedness! It's true that if we make up our minds to do something, we usually get it done. It may not always happen the way we figured it would, but it gets accomplished. And it's a little hard to talk us out of something if we've decided to do it.

Over the years we've had our share of arguments around home. We each voice our opinions, but we're usually able to talk things out so we get along pretty well.

My mother is a Zook and, in addition to being a determined family also, they do well at expressing things they feel deeply.

Those two streams of qualities have produced interesting combinations in us brothers!

Growing up was a happy time because we did a lot of things together. We had strong traditions—going to the mountains on at least two different weekends during the summer, and spending a week at the shore.

The one weekend in the mountains was a King gathering and the other was always a Kennel get-together for a part of my mother's family. Some of our Kennel cousins lived in Indiana so those two-day vacations were really special. Our week at the ocean we usually spent with others in the King clan, so we were surrounded by family. In fact, Mom and Dad both grew up at Maple Grove Mennonite Church and they also went to school together. Both sets of my grandparents knew each other well!

Our farm work kept us close home, so I remember clearly the only two long trips we took before I was in high school—we visited the World's Fair when it was in New York and we went to Florida for Christmas to see Mom's aunt, when I was in third grade. Somewhere I got the itch to travel and took off to Europe with two friends right after our high school graduation.

Dad helped us learn to play ball, but he and Mom also taught us to sing. The two of them sang a lot, sometimes as part of a quartet in church, sometimes with other groups. Mom was part of a trio with her sister and Dad's sister. And different members of the King family used to travel around to churches in the local area, giving music programs.

I remember that at Christmas and Easter, before we were old enough to help with the outdoor work, Mom and Dad would come in from the barn in the morning and we had to wait upstairs until we heard them singing. They had been spreading our Christmas presents under the tree, and at Easter time, hiding our baskets while all was quiet. Their singing was our signal to come down!

Going to church was simply part of life. We always went on Sunday mornings and usually attended the Wednesday evening midweek meetings. Dad's been active at Maple Grove in Christian education for many years, as a Sunday school teacher and superintendent.

When I got older I taught summer Bible school, ushered, and

sang. In my senior year of high school I was president of the youth group. I felt I couldn't be a song leader, though when I was asked. I didn't feel qualified, but more than that, I was very quiet and reserved in front of people. Before my accident I wasn't nearly as outgoing as I am now.

High school was an obligation I had to fulfill, so I concentrated on succeeding in sports rather than making good grades. I did okay in my classes but I didn't exactly strive since I figured college wasn't for me. I liked to sing so I joined Campus Chorale, but my heart was in cross-country. That was the sport I excelled in, although I played some soccer and basketball.

I went to our local public high school until the end of my sophomore year. Then I transferred to Lancaster Mennonite High School, and overlapped one year there with my older brother Rodney. He left for college the fall after he graduated, so Curt and I became much closer brothers. I was then the oldest boy at home, and he and I worked together out in the barn. I played a lot of ice hockey the next two years and Curt often came to watch. I also introduced him to snow skiing and water skiing. In fact, those three sports were at the top of my list when I left on the motorcycle trip on August 6, 1978.

Fixing My Back

I thought Dr. Schwentker was a mean doctor. He stood in my room at Hershey Medical, reading my chart, throwing medical terms at me that were supposed to explain what was wrong with my back. I didn't really understand, and he looked at me finally and asked me if I knew what my condition was.

"You probably will never walk again," he said straight out.

I just didn't know what to say. It was tough having a doctor bring the news that way because none of the doctors in Calgary had ever said it. I really didn't like this guy.

Dr. Dystra, who had come along with us from Foothills, spent two days with Dr. Schwentker explaining their medical procedure to him and showing what they had found. For about a week they took X-rays and generally checked me out. Then they were ready to operate. The Hershey people had already invested some energy in me; they had medically overseen my flights home. Dan Wert, a friend of my aunt's, was an anesthesiologist at the Medical Center. He came in the morning of my surgery to explain what was about to happen. I was pretty doped up when I rolled into the operating room but I noticed them wrapping up a table. I glanced at Dr. Schwentker, who was looking at me, and I asked, "Are you guys going to put me on that?" It was different than I had expected to see. I remember Dr. Schwentker telling them to put me out, and before I knew it I was gone.

They laid me, stomach down, on a table that had four pads, two for my shoulders to rest on, and two that supported me at the bottom of my rib cage. The thing was built so my hips didn't lie on anything and my backbone was in its natural straight position.

The operation was to repair the vertebrae that had been crushed when I hit the car. Bones they can fix; spinal cords they can't.

They made a nearly twenty-inch long incision, then stretched the skin back to have just enough room to reach into my backbone and work around it. They had to bare the whole section so they could first insert bone chips from my hip, wrap them in wire, and then put in two Harrington rods, one on each side of my backbone, to hold everything in place until the bone knit together.

The Harrington rods are still back there. I don't need them anymore, but removing them would be a major item, so they'll stay unless they cause a problem.

The six-inch section of my backbone that was broken is now a solid bone instead of the smaller jointed pieces that were there before. But I have enough flexibility to comfortably move around and bend down to pick something up.

Fusing my backbone together was an eight-hour operation. I could tell I had been on the table awhile because when I woke up my shoulders and ribs were terribly sore from having supported my weight for so long.

Had they tried to fix my spinal cord, I'd have been on that table for weeks! First of all, my spinal cord was simply gone in that area where the vertebrae had been crushed. It was completely done away with by the impact of the accident. But had it all been there, the doctors would still not have been able to reattach it. They said it would be like cutting a high tension cable apart, and then trying to match up all the many little wires inside it with their right ends. It would be nearly impossible to connect them all back together correctly.

When it was all over and I was back in the recovery room, they kept trying to wake me up and I kept telling them to let me sleep. I didn't like the burning sensation I felt along my center back each time I roused. When I finally did come out of my anesthesia it felt like someone was running a hot knife down my back where they had made the incision.

That was the first real pain I felt since being hurt. When I woke up in Calgary the first night after the accident I had no pain at all. I was uncomfortable because of all the tubes in me, but this was something different. I was given medication to dull the pain and when it was almost time for the next dose, I always definitely asked for another shot.

I stayed groggy for awhile and didn't always know what was going on around me. I do remember though, that friends dropped in to stay with me for short times. I'd say "Hi" and "Goodbye," and then go out again like a light.

In about two weeks my incision healed enough so that I was ready to start rehabilitation at the Elizabethtown Hospital. The Hershey team fitted me in a body cast and transferred me to Eileen Tymon and her rehab team. I was officially a paraplegic, without the use of my legs and without muscle control below my belly button. I was not a quadriplegic without the use of my upper body. Thankfully I had strength and the ability to move everything from my waist up.

No Call Buttons

Elizabethtown Rehab Center depressed me a lot when I first got there. It didn't look like a hospital. And they didn't have call buttons so you had to yell for a nurse.

I discovered there were two reasons for that—it *was* an old building, but having no call buttons was also a technique in our rehabilitation. I faced a drastic change coming from Foothills Hospital and Hershey Medical Center to Elizabethtown. At the other two hospitals, I pushed the button, the nurse came, I told her what I wanted, she got it for me. That's the way it was and that's the way I expected it to be at E-town. That switch was the start of my facing up to what life from then on would be like.

Once I was able to get up and out of bed myself I found that if

I asked the staff for something they'd say, "You know where it is. Get it yourself!" That threw me for a real loop because I figured people were supposed to pity me and get me whatever I needed! I know now it did me a lot of good, because it got me started at being independent.

Gradually the environment helped me, and I learned to like the people. Eileen Tymon was the head coordinator at Elizabethtown. A registered nurse, she was in charge of rehabilitation programs for patients with spinal cord injuries. The first time I met her I could tell she was concerned about me as a person. She's warm, she's pretty, she has a good sense of humor. And I found her comfortable to talk to.

All that mattered a lot because rehab isn't easy. I needed to know that I had someone behind me that was going to work with me the whole way.

Fortunately she hadn't gotten impatient with me and my family when we were still at the Foothills Hospital trying to plan for my care in Pennsylvania! Dad had been given the name and number of a person at Hershey who could advise us, and each time he'd try to reach the guy a woman would answer and offer to help. Dad was getting frustrated and kept hanging up on her, until they finally talked awhile one day, only to have Dad discover that this person who kept answering the phone was the specialist he was looking for! That was Eileen's first encounter with us!

Never did I feel she wanted to get rid of me to make room for someone else. But I knew she wanted to have me rehabilitated so I could get on with my life.

I lived in an olive green room with three other people. And although what I saw out the window was pretty country, I spent as little time in my room as possible. When I wasn't in physical therapy, which took most of the mornings and afternoons, I'd go to the lounge to play games or watch TV.

Six of us, who had experienced spinal cord injuries within two weeks of each other, went through rehab together. The five guys and one girl were all from central Pennsylvania; three of us were paraplegics; the other three were quadriplegics.

I don't keep in regular contact with them now, but when I go back for my clinic visits, I always ask the Elizabethtown staff about each one, where they are and what they're doing. I had hoped to meet them all again on my trip this summer, but saw just two of them when I came into Hershey and E-town. Going through rehab as part of a group beat doing it alone. We joked around, encouraged each other, and even got competitive, trying to outdo each other in weight-lifting and generally just regaining strength.

When I came to E-town I was in a body cast that started right under my arms and ran down to my hips. After wearing that for about three weeks I was fitted for a plastic clam shell jacket that I could take off and on. I was finally able to shower rather than have sponge baths in bed!

They wakened us at seven o'clock each morning, then served us breakfast in our rooms. I usually ate cereal because I wasn't very hungry. Before my accident I weighed about 175 pounds, but I lost twenty pounds during my hospitalizations before beginning rehab.

Then after a bath I headed down to therapy. At first two aides, Debby Miller and Janet Houseal, took me in my bed because my legs couldn't bend. Betty Husted, the therapist, worked at loosening up the muscles in my lower extremities by doing "range of motion" exercises. My knees were stiff and wouldn't give beyond a thirty degree angle, so she slowly stretched them out, gradually loosening them. It hurt, but I didn't feel it!

She also flexed my hip joints and ankles. Before starting any of this, and as I progressed, Betty tested each part of me from head to foot to see how limber I was and what kind of muscle tone and muscle movement I had. Those tests showed that my upper body was okay and that most of the work needed to be done from my hips down.

These people obviously knew what they were doing! If someone had grabbed my legs and yanked away, they'd have torn muscles or ligaments or broken a bone.

While Betty worked with my legs, she'd give me weights and barbells to lift so I could begin strengthening my arms and shoulders and getting my muscle tone back. I had lost so much of that during the weeks I lay in the hospitals.

At 11:30 the aides took me upstairs for lunch and at one o'clock rolled me back down again for more work. We had fun in therapy. They kept us busy, but it wasn't like a military drill! Music played,

Album Two: Accident and Recovery

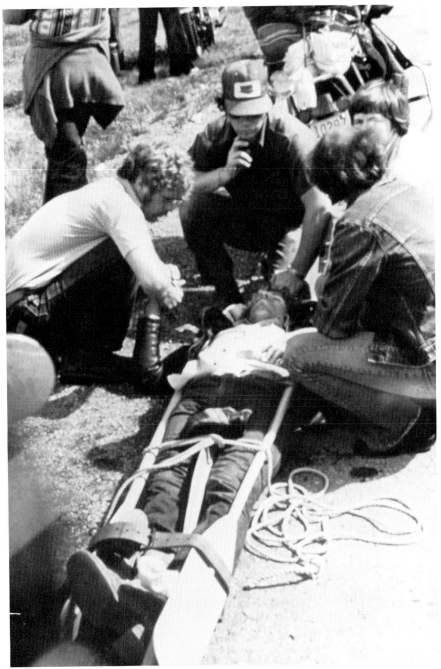

This is a scene of the accident.

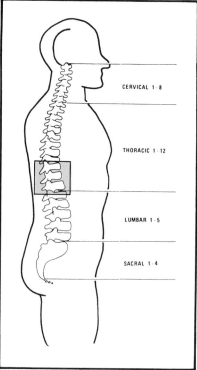

CERVICAL 1 - 8

THORACIC 1 - 12

LUMBAR 1 - 5

SACRAL 1 - 4

Mom and Dad catch some fresh air with me during those three weeks at the Foothills Hospital in Calgary, Alberta.

The spinal column consists of 29 vertebrae. The three vertebrae indicated by the box (T 10-12) were crushed in my accident. This left me a paraplegic. I have no muscle control from my belly button on down. (If my injury had occured at T-1 or above, I would have been a quadriplegic.)

Dr. Schwentker, my surgeon at Hershey Medical, and Eileen Tymon, former head coordinator of Elizabethtown Rehabilitation Hospital, (seen here with me when I passed through Hershey on my cross-country trip).

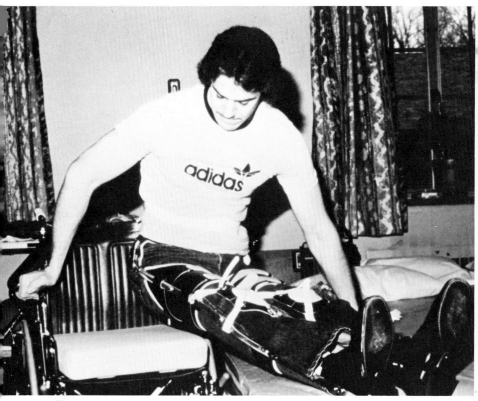

Here are several scenes from my rehabilitation at Elizabethtown Hospital. Developing strength and muscles in my upper body was very important. The staff were really helpful.

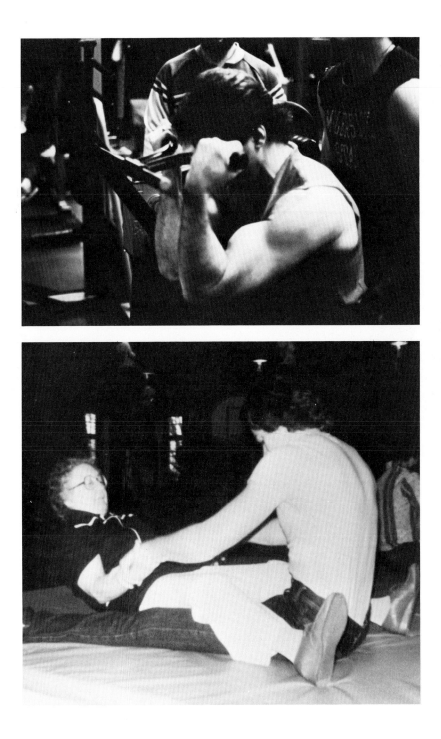

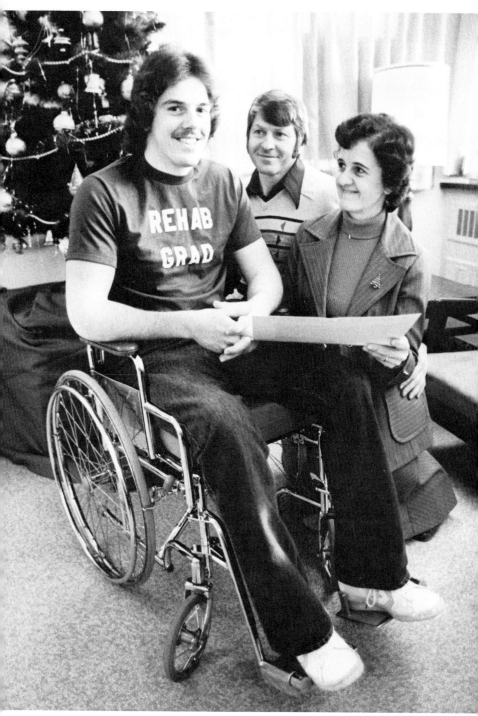

The day I was discharged from Elizabethtown Rehab Center.

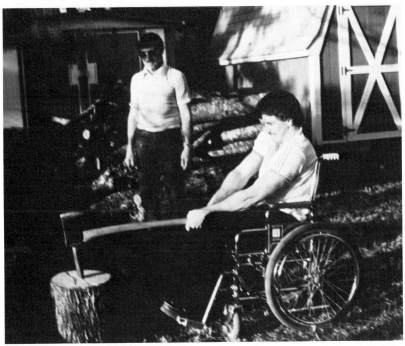

I even learned to chop wood!

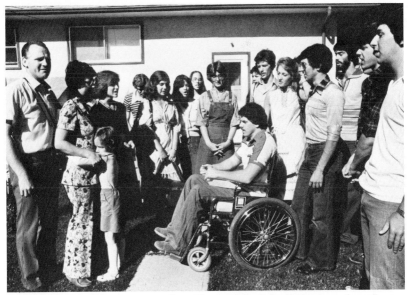

This was taken a year after the accident in Calgary when I was on tour with Choraleers. Jacob Wiebe (far left) and his family had supported my family and me so much during the weeks after the accident.

During the summer of 1979 (for two weeks) and the spring of 1980 (for four months), I traveled with the youth choir, Choraleers, in music ministry throughout the States, Canada, and Central America.

we tried all kinds of stuff, and always had jokes going. When I was able to sit up in a wheelchair and get in and out of it myself, the aides no longer needed to take me up and down to therapy. I learned to use the parallel bars to stand myself up or do push-ups. And I'd strap myself into the machine that would stand me up by locking my legs and hips into an upright position. That was a good way to relieve the tiredness of sitting so much. We didn't work constantly downstairs. Sometimes I just sat and talked. Other times I played around on my own with all kinds of equipment. The range and intensity of my exercises increased as I was ready. Eileen and Betty told me that the faster I learned how to do living techniques and completed my physical workouts, the sooner I'd get out of the place. I was pretty well fed up with hospitals by then so I worked hard at it and finished rehab in a little over two months, rather than the usual three or four months.

For instance, once I was able to sit up in my wheelchair all day long, I started increasing the weights I was lifting. I'd sort of jump myself out of my chair over onto the mat where I could stretch out my leg muscles. And I learned how to take care of myself so I can now live alone. For example, my shower is equipped with a stool I can sit on, and I've figured out how to put on my pants either in bed or on my chair.

Therapy ended at 3:30 and we were free to hang around until dinner time at five o'clock. Sometimes I went outside in the fall afternoons, and nearly every evening someone came to visit me.

Before I went on the cycle trip I had sung with the Choraleers, a music group of Mennonite teenagers who had been students at Lancaster Mennonite High School. Our 1978 season had ended in the spring before I left, but Arnold Moshier, the director, had invited me to begin again in the fall. Well, my plans changed! But Arnold decided to keep his end of the bargain. Frequently during those weeks when I was at E-town, he would drive up from Lancaster and take me down to his home for rehearsal. I didn't begin singing with the group until the spring of 1979, but he wanted me to be able to learn to know the new kids and hear the new music!

I saw Dr. Schwentker on a good many of the evenings. A number of his surgical patients were in rehab at E-town, so he made rounds with us when he finished his day at Hershey. By then I knew he was a good doctor! I saw him for check-ups after I was discharged and I can call him anytime now if I have problems. When we put together our Hope for Life board of directors, I wanted him there!

When I left Elizabethtown on December 15, 1978, my physical condition was much improved from when I had come three months earlier. But inside I hadn't begun to heal.

How My Family Took It All

Greg Petersheim had called my folks at about 10 o'clock, the August Sunday night of my accident, while I was in the Foothills operating room. He didn't know a lot of specifics then, but promised to call them back as soon as he had more information.

Mom and Dad got their tickets the next morning and flew right out to Calgary. It wasn't until they were in the Foothills Hospital that Dr. Dystra and Dr. Cochran told them the extent of my injuries.

Of course, a dairy farm needs constant care. So my brothers and some other family picked up on a lot of the work around home so my folks could be with me the three weeks I was hospitalized in Calgary.

I know the whole thing was tough on my dad. I think he was like I was—wanting to deny what had happened. He didn't want to believe that one of his sons was handicapped for life.

Mom is more talkative and has always been more able to express her feelings, so from the beginning she would ask me questions and tell me how she felt.

For several years after the accident, Dad and I couldn't talk to each other about what had happened. He wasn't sure how to treat me.

Back then, I didn't even know myself how I wanted to be treated! And my feelings about that kept changing. We had a hard time communicating within our family during those days. None of us five brothers find it easy to talk about our feelings. And we all wondered how things were going to be, how to relate to each other, what to say.

After I was in rehab at the Elizabethtown Hospital, Curt would often come to see me or he'd pick me up and take me out for the evening.

None of them ever avoided me. They'd joke around with me. Every chance they got, they'd come to see me. And when I came home on weekends they would help me up the steps. But we didn't talk about what I was going through inside.

There was a big change for all of us when I moved home from the hospital. Since things weren't yet set up for me I had to have help getting into the house. I had to have help getting out of the house. And I couldn't get upstairs to my bedroom.

At first they all catered to me! I'd ask for something and they'd go and get it for me. In time they learned to put things they knew I needed at my level. Then when I'd ask them to get something for me, they'd look at me like, "Who do you think you are?" Naturally they wanted to help me and they pitied me, but that soon got old. I know I took advantage of them often when I could have done something myself.

As time went on and I became more independent, I realized a lot of satisfaction in accomplishing things. I stopped asking my family to do everything for me. When I learned that making other people miserable didn't make me feel any better, I started doing things for myself.

Now I know what I can do. And I know when I need to ask for

help. My brothers and my folks understand that.

Our house has changed to accommodate me. We built an addition that we had been thinking about for some time. It includes not only a larger family room, but my bedroom and bath on the first floor. So I don't need to go upstairs anymore, unless I want to just see what it looks like. But I haven't been up in the last four years!

And we kind of remodeled our kitchen so the cereal and some of the food is within my reach where I can help myself to it.

Probably the best development of all is the good feeling we have within our family. I think all the guys are glad to be my brothers. I know I'm proud to be theirs.

Deciding To Live

There are certain things you can't hurry. I had pushed my body through therapy, but my spirit was a different matter.

When I moved home, my bedroom was still upstairs. A lot of times I refused to come downstairs for two- and three-day stretches. Sometimes I felt so sorry for myself I stayed in bed all day long. I simply didn't feel like getting up. I cried, and I wanted other people to pity me too.

Mom brought food up to me. I wasn't very hungry but I did eat. (In fact, until I went on the wheelchair trip, I usually ate only one meal a day.)

Finally after about a month of that I went back to work in February for Steven Smoker, the building contractor I was with before my accident. Earlier I worked on his framing crew; now he gave me an office job doing drafting which I had first learned in high school, and got better acquainted with when I had to read blueprints on the job.

Steven built mostly private homes. People would come in with a picture of the house they liked and the general layout they wanted. I'd sketch up a few preliminary plans and review them with the couple, they'd choose the final floor plan, and I'd do a refined drawing for the carpenter crew to build. Steven did some commercial buildings also, in much the same way, except they always required state approval.

Any new commercial building must be handicap-accessible. Usually there was at least one step up into a proposed building, and even though that would have passed, I knew it was a difficult maneuver for someone in a wheelchair. Often doorways were drawn too narrow for my chair to have gone through. So it was kind of funny to have people come in who were quite cost-conscious, but then they'd see me and kind of change things around a little! Usually they'd suggest making the door slightly bigger or cutting the curb or adding a ramp!

I liked the job, but being inside all the time bothered me. I'm an outdoors person.

I started singing again with Choraleers in the spring of 1979, soon after coming home from Elizabethtown. Arnold's having stayed in touch with me during my physical therapy was the key to my deciding to sing again with the group in church programs. Arnold had never worked with anyone in a wheelchair, so he just asked a lot of questions about how I was doing, without waiting for me to offer things about myself. I found him an easy guy to talk to. And that whole experience helped me to begin to crawl out of my sadness and anger.

It's true that with the singing group I had bad times and good times. I got a lot of attention. Sometimes I just wished people would leave me alone. I didn't like a big deal being made that I was there and singing, in spite of being in a wheelchair. But that was part of what I bit off when I began again with Choraleers.

In August of 1979 after several months as a draftsman for Steven, I took a vacation so I could join the Choraleers for their two-week summer tour. I wanted to do it even though I wasn't sure what traveling in a wheelchair would be like. And, of course, I didn't know what trouble I might have. We flew to San Francisco, then drove back through the northwest provinces and states.

Naturally I had a lot of physical limitations but two of my good friends, Jay Embleton and Tim Lapp, were also in the group and they had learned to pull me up and down steps. At first they were a little shaky about it although it isn't that hard. Soon it got to be really routine and one of them would whip me up and down stairs as quickly as someone could walk them.

Times went well on the trip in spite of minor difficulties. And in late August, exactly one year after my accident, we were back on Alberta's Highway 1A between Banff and Lake Louise. It was a freaky experience. The weather conditions were the same as that earlier August—kind of chilly and rainy.

Greg Petersheim was in the music group too, and I asked him to show me exactly where my accident had happened. But a mile away from where I had been hurt, we came upon an accident that had traffic so backed up we couldn't pass the site. We sang that evening at First Mennonite Church in Calgary. After the program I heard on the news that six people were involved in the accident we had passed earlier on Highway 1A. None of them had survived.

Greg and I spent the night at the Penners, the same family who had hosted Greg and Merv Stoltzfus one year ago. We were telling each other what we remembered thinking the August before, and Greg said that when I was in the operating room and the staff were saying they didn't know if I was going to make it, he felt God telling him I would be all right, that someday I was going to walk again.

From then on I've had a hope that I will walk sometime in the future. I know that medically it's an impossibility, but I believe God could help me step out of my chair. What's more, when I think of those six people who died near where I was hurt, I wonder why I'm still alive.

Things changed for me after that night near Calgary. I began to believe I was here for a purpose and I decided to let God use me in the best way he can. If it's in a wheelchair, fine. But I know when he can use me better out of the chair, he'll help me walk.

Album Three: College and Travel

Visiting Seaworld in Amsterdam, Holland, while touring Europe in 1976 with friends Myron Stoltzfus and Don Shenk.

I always loved to ski.
With traveling in my blood, I did as much as I could afford. Below is a shot of me on the cycle trip in Wisconsin.

Above is the crew I worked with while at Hesston College (the yearbook staff).

Below is a scene from my trip to Brazil.

(Above) I tried my luck at arm wrestling while in the Midwest. I won this match, but lost later to the Kansas State Champion. Music, being a big part of my life, I traveled with Parousia (below), a seven-person group, for the summers of '82 and '83.

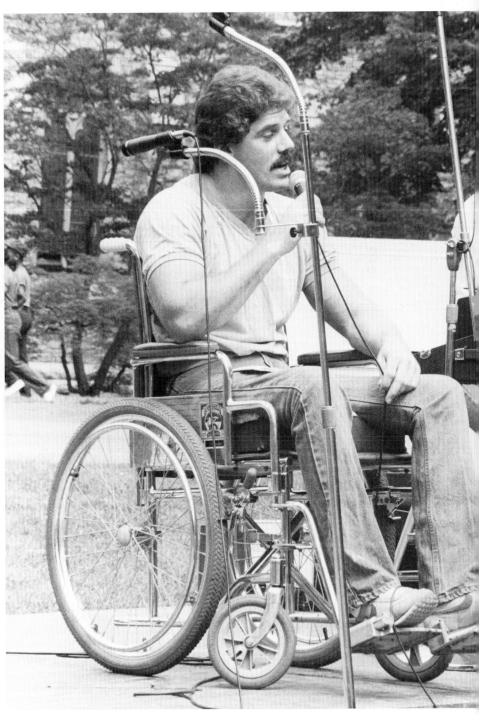

A picture of me singing at "Bethlehem 83" Youth Convention.

I finished my education at Tabor College and, yes, I did graduate, along with housemates Doug Peachey and Ken Weaver!

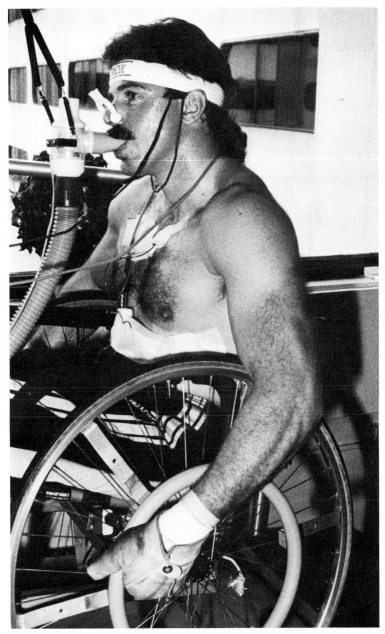

The Hershey Medical Center put me through "Energetic Testing" to see if I could take the trip. At first we all wondered if I had the stamina to complete the trip, but they said I passed with flying colors, and termed me a "superbly fine-tuned athlete."

***This was the first Associated Press publicity shot taken in a town
near my home. It looks like I'm passing the Amish buggy, but in fact
the buggy was slowly gaining on me.***

From then on my positive times outweighed my down times. Before that, it was certainly the other way around! I was better able to accept my situation. And I started to think about building up my life again, finding something worthwhile to do.

Because I have no memory of the accident itself I'm able to go back to the place where it happened without reservation. I've been there five times since I was hurt and each time I have good feelings. I think it's because of the warm people who are there, who worked with us and cared for us. Going to Calgary is always a special experience for me. I like the folks and the countryside!

Our Choraleers tour continued. Because of my presence, Arnold scheduled programs in retirement homes, hospitals, and rehab centers. I was glad to be able to visit with others who had physical disabilities. After I left E-town, I saw almost no one in my regular circles who had a visible handicap.

Then in December 1979, Choraleers were due to begin their four-month cross-country tour. The two-week stint with the group had gone well, so I decided to go again.

There is a two-year Mennonite college on the plains of central Kansas, in the small town of Hesston. My brother Rod had gone there and liked it, so when we came through the area during the last month of the tour, I gathered up information about the place, talked with the registrar's office, and pretty well decided I'd come back to school in the fall.

The springtime tour had been a real turning point for me. I came home to work, drawing kitchen designs part-time for a cabinet craftsman. I also started leading a few Bible studies with youth groups. That's when I got the idea to major in youth ministries at Hesston.

All of that was quite a twist from the way I had expected my life to be! I went through high school taking just what I needed because I knew college wasn't for me. I planned to be a farmer.

When I left on the cycle trip I assumed I'd come back and go into business with Dad on our dairy farm. Milking cows wasn't the fun part, but I liked field work and driving tractor. I enjoyed helping Dad and working around home.

Even after I had another job, I'd get up and milk in the morning before I left for the day. And if Dad was still out in the barn when I got home, I'd sometimes go out and help him finish up.

I still love farming and every chance I get I help with the field work. Our farm machinery dealer rigged a set of hand controls for our tractor, so I can and do drive.

College, Too

Going to college began to seem natural after I got restless drafting blueprints and after I had done some traveling and speaking. My accident had made me vulnerable and I was learning to be more open with people. Churches were asking me to lead weekend retreats with their youth groups, and I was looking for resource and a broader view of the world.

Hesston was the first place I would live, apart from home, since my accident. Lauren Martin became my roommate. In fact, it was he who finally convinced me to try school. We first learned to know each other in Choraleers after I was hurt. He came to visit me at Elizabethtown and let me know he had no idea what to do, but he wanted to help in any way he could. After that, he just seemed to be around whenever I needed him!

So I became the first wheelchair student to live at Hesston College. Lauren used to come back to our room and say, "This guy was asking me about you. He wants to know how to come up and talk to you!" I thought it was kind of funny. I learned when I sensed someone was uneasy around me to just say, "Hey, I'm a normal person. And I'm not mad about my disability!" That usually relaxed things and triggered questions about what had happened.

Once students at Hesston got to know me, they treated me like everyone else. No more walking out around a different way so they wouldn't have to go by me! In fact, we came up with a lot of wheelchair jokes.

I wasn't on campus long before I learned I was the cause of a kind of major debate within the administrative staff. Most of the buildings at Hesston hold their main activities on their first floors. But not all places I needed to go were accessible to me. They made a few minor changes in my dorm bathroom and put in some curb cuts and ramps elsewhere, but the more extensive renovations became a real issue.

I never pushed the matter. In fact, I felt almost guilty for choosing to go there because my presence and my need raised the issue. My profs were advocates of the changes. But I sensed that administrative people, who knew things weren't set up properly, held me at arm's length so they wouldn't become emotionally involved with me. Some of them argued that if they made changes to accommodate a person in a wheelchair, they'd have to offer everything in Braille so a blind student could get along at Hesston, too.

One day Lauren and I met for lunch as usual. There were about ten steps down to the cafeteria so I depended on Lauren's help to get me there. That noon, a few steps from the bottom, his feet slipped and the two of us fell the rest of the way, right into the cafeteria, and right in front of a major contributor to the College, who happened to be eating there that day. Within a few weeks, a ramp was installed at the entrance to the cafeteria.

But that uneasy matter didn't cloud my years there. I joined Parousia, a music group, and toured with them through the school year to surrounding communities. And during the summers of 1982 and 1983 we travelled from Florida to Pennsylvania to Colorado and back. Music sort of replaced athletics for me after my accident, especially in college. While the sports teams were out practicing, I had choir rehearsal. I'm sure that if I could have played sports, I wouldn't have sung in the music groups. I spent the summer of 1981, between my two years at Hesston, traveling nearly every weekend to youth groups. So I felt my training was paying off. But when I went back to Elizabethtown in August for my annual check-up, an idea that had barely formed in my mind began to take shape. One of the staff who knew me asked whether I was planning to come back there to work. A handicapped person would be an ideal counsellor to disabled people, as could an able-bodied person with lots of exposure to those individuals and their particular needs.

The question was well-timed. I liked the experiences and exposure to the Bible which my church ministries studies were giving me. But that program wouldn't give me the credentials I needed to work with the handicapped. I began to think seriously about going on for a social work degree so I could be employed by a rehab hospital.

Tabor College, also located in central Kansas, also operated by a Mennonite denomination, ranks as high in social work training in the state of Kansas as does Kansas University. It was a natural choice for me as the place to complete my four-year degree. (Being a graduate of Tabor later helped me to be accepted in the University of Pennsyvlania's social work graduate program.)

The first few weeks at Tabor were a replay of my early days at Hesston. Once again, people got sort of stiff when I showed up, until they got used to me! Tabor had had one wheelchair student many years earlier, so I raised all the accessibility questions again.

I'm gone from both Hesston and Tabor now, and I can't help but wonder how many changes they will continue to make, at their own initiative.

The state of Kansas prides itself in the establishing of facilities for the handicapped. Senator Robert Dole, who has a disability himself, is from Kansas and has worked hard at that effort. For instance, when I was at Tabor they built an addition to the library, and to meet regulations they had to put in an elevator to the second floor. They are presently building a new fine arts center and that will have to be accessible by elevator. And when they began renovating some rooms on the second floor of their three-story administration building, they were required to make the whole place handicap-accessible.

When I graduated from Tabor in May of 1984, Senator Dole attended the ceremonies and congratulated me, recognizing my efforts in school despite my disability. It was a pleasure meeting a Senator personally, especially because he had some sense of the path I had come.

Getting Along Without Working Legs

Funny things happen in your head when you lose the use of your legs!

During those first few years, I saw only a dim future full of a lot of questions. Who was I, really? Why did this happen to me? What was I going to do with myself?

Certain things were clear. Physically, I was without feeling from my belly button on down. I have some skin sensation in that area, but then it drops off quickly. Internally I can sense pressure on my lower abdomen. And if my legs get bumped hard I feel the bone vibrating, but I have no skin sensation on my feet and legs.

My muscles still work, so that if something hot gets against my legs, the muscles go crazy. But I don't feel the pain. The coordination, the signal to the muscle to move, isn't there, but if I cross my legs and someone hits my knee, the reflexes respond. Before the accident my feet were terribly ticklish. Now if I rub the bottom of my foot lightly, my toes twitch wildly! At night in bed I lie there and mentally wiggle my big toe and my ankle, and bend my knees up to my chest. My brain sends the signals out, but they never go further than my belly button since that's the level at which my spinal cord is severed. So, even though I can get up and walk around in my mind, the message never gets to my legs.

Thankfully my arms work well, so at night if I want to change my position while sleeping, I just reach up, grab the headboard on my bed and pull myself over. Or if I sit all day, like I did on the twenty-four-hour drive to and from school to Kansas, my back gets tight so I lie down for awhile. I also have a set of braces I can stand up in, just to change positions.

Lauren Martin, who was with me on the wheelchair trip, learned, when he was my roommate at Hesston, to help me relieve my back tension. I pull myself up into a standing position and he grabs my knees and holds them. We did that on the road this summer after I'd have a long workout in my chair.

Six weeks after my release from Elizabethtown I started driving again. I didn't know anything about hand controls on vehicles until an instructor at E-town introduced me to the possibilities in a car they had there. In fact, most people who have had spinal cord injuries can drive if they want to. Quadriplegics have all kinds of gadgets available to them—hydraulics, for example, that respond to light arm or foot or head movements.

Getting back in my Chevy Blazer was good for me. I bought hand controls from a man in Lancaster who was a paraplegic and happened to have an extra set, so I avoided the long wait of ordering them from the manufacturer, and I installed them myself.

The controls attach to the steering column and work on a ratchet system. There is only one lever and it makes the foot pedals operate—if I pull it toward my lap, the accelerator kicks in; if I push it away from myself, the brake is engaged. Anyone can drive the same vehicle by just ignoring the hand controls and using the pedals.

Album Four: Alaska and the Yukon

This was my first sight of the mountains, after leaving North Pole,
Alaska. I was wondering if I had to cross that mountain!

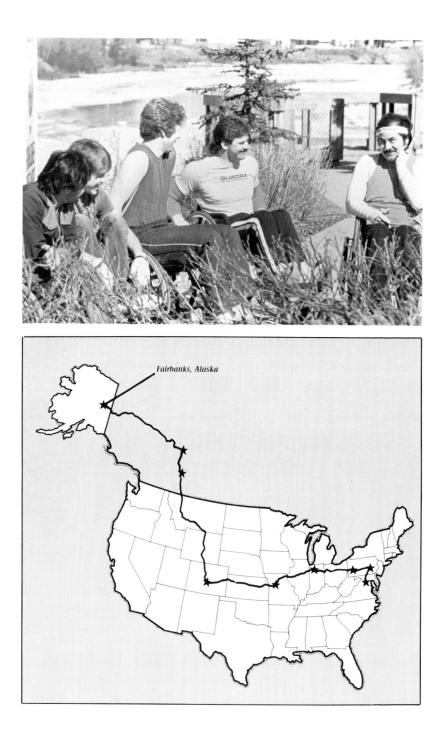

Fairbanks, Alaska

(Upper left) The 4 people who participated with me in the 15-mile race that started my trip. I came in third. Of course, I had 40 more miles to put in!

(Lower left) A map of our trip. All 5600 miles of it.

(Above) Delta Junction is a very memorable place for me, where some high schoolers asked if they could bike with me.

The Alaskan Highway is very unique. Where possible, airplanes are allowed to land. Here Don Shenk and friends flew down to "1260 Mile Post" to spend with us our last night in Alaska.

Gloves were important; without them my hands would have looked like raw meat. Putting them on properly was important to keep from getting blisters.

When the dust was too bad, I became "the masked man," in order that the air I breathed was a bit cleaner.

(Below) My first experience of rainy weather crossing Trutch Mountain, B.C. The storm was followed by a rainbow.

Trucks make up the majority of traffic on the Alaskan Highway, making their weekly or daily trips up and down the road. I was glad they slowed down their rigs on the gravel stretches.

Just one of the beautiful modern structures in the beauty of nature (Laird River, B.C.).

And I enjoy taking care of my truck. I have a little cart I can lie on and scoot underneath to change the oil. Getting in and out of the truck isn't a problem. When I'm by myself I crawl in on the passenger side, fold my chair, slide over to the driver's side, and pull the chair up. If someone's with me they just throw the chair in the back of the truck.

In time I got my appetite back. I like to eat, especially Pennsylvania Dutch cooking—meat and potatoes combinations, with ham loaf or chicken or roast beef or steak! I steer away from desserts, except ice cream. I always eat a lot of that!

From the start of the trauma until now, my friends have always stood beside me. And the church supported both me and my family. The one guy who went through rehab with me lost some of his friends when he became disabled. They simply didn't know how to relate to him. That's one loss I've never suffered. In fact many of my friendships are stronger. My friends helped me find a new life, and I believe I've shown them a new outlook.

My home church congregation at Maple Grove took a special offering for us that we used to pay medical expenses that my health insurance didn't cover. (Insurance did pay for my first wheelchair.) Two friends in Lac La Bich, Alberta, paid for the six air tickets we needed from Calgary to Harrisburg. But we had no assistance, other than borrowing from the bank, to foot the sizable bills for building a first-floor bedroom and bath for me. I received workman's compensation for six weeks, and after that Social Security picked up. I'll continue to receive those payments until I finish school and begin working again.

I've had a lot of time to think these last seven years, and even though some questions still have no answers, I have made a lot of peace.

I am more sure of my faith. I'm not embarrassed about what I believe and I'm strong enough now not to be swayed. I used to be ashamed of being a Mennonite, depending where I went. Kids at my public high school made fun of the way I talked sometimes and called me "a little Mennonite boy" or "Yonie," to show how backward they thought I was.

I've liked being identified with Mennonites in the years since I was hurt—from the Wiebes and Penners who cared for my family and friends in Calgary, to the folks at Maple Grove who helped bring me up, then stepped in with concrete care when we needed it most.

I didn't travel 5600 miles in a wheelchair without a lot of prayers—my own, and the church community's. I reached down deep inside over and over again this summer to find a source that would help me over literal mountains, through sweaty hot humidity, and all that with blistered raw hands.

It's not a false hope I have or a denial of the truth about my physical condition, but I want Christ to use me in the best way he can. That goal gives me peace.

In fact, it helps me ask my old struggling questions in a new way. I often wonder, why did I get hurt and not one of the other three guys? When I was born, was I predestined to have this accident? Why me and not someone else?

I've finally decided that those questions simply have no answers. For at least two years I was angry about all of that. Now I still wonder, but I have a new question: Why not me? It has taken time and emotional strength to get that question rephrased.

I don't believe God caused my accident. I don't think he's above us pointing his finger at every little turn we're supposed to take. I think he is with us though, as a guiding person. But we make choices about what we want to do. I decided to go on the cycle trip. I failed to notice the car. It's not God's fault or anyone else's.

Without other people of faith supporting and encouraging me, however, I may never have turned my plaguing questions around.

My friends and family who helped me most were willing to let me be depressed. They weren't threatened by my anger and they put up with my nasty moods.

In fact, as a result of all this, I'm better able to handle my feelings than before the accident. The whole healing process and my years in college have helped me express myself a little more healthfully. I used to really bottle things up inside, then all of a sudden let them blow up on someone else. Now I vent my feelings a lot more. It's still easy for me to keep things to myself, but I no longer wait until I'm tight to let them out. I've learned to talk to myself, and especially to friends, about the way I feel.

Unfortunately, some people weren't quite as patient with my family. Dad's feelings about my accident were similar to my own.

Naturally, he was upset. His son was disabled for life. He was angry at God and other people for what had happened to me. And it was perfectly normal for him to feel like that.

But that's not what he heard. He was told it wasn't right for him to have those feelings. So on top of his grief and disappointment, he was given a load of guilt. All of that only made his working through his frustrations take a lot longer. Somehow people could accept my bitterness as a "stage" or figured I didn't really mean it, but they couldn't quite offer that grace to my family.

Venting my anger let me more quickly get back in touch with the person I was inside. When I began to see myself again, and really believe I was the same person, despite my physical handicap, my mind and spirit began to be healed.

That's when I began to think of the things I *could* do rather than the things I *couldn't* do. Since I was a little kid, I've always wanted to do everything possible. That hasn't changed, but I don't take things for granted anymore—like being able to get up and go somewhere and run around, and never before my accident did I give thanks for the use of my upper body!

Maybe it was a symbol of the new health I felt. Maybe it was just my old wanderlust that hadn't been dimmed by my accident, but in January of 1983, during our interterm at Tabor, I went to visit my cousin, Kevin King, who was working in Brazil. He was there on a three-year assignment in agricultural production under Mennonite Central Committee, a worldwide relief and service organization.

I've always liked traveling and at first thought I might work to earn college credits for the month-long inland tour of Brazil. But I decided instead to just enjoy the country and learn what I could about the people and Kevin's work.

I've flown alone domestically, but never out of the country. So I invited Lauren Martin to join me. I'd have still gone, had he not been able to, since Kevin picked us up at the airport and did all the driving. We met Brazilian farmers who were experimenting with crop irrigation at Kevin's suggestion. And we visited villages where he was digging wells in an effort to find pure drinking water. We vacationed on the beach, took a cruise, and drove to the city of Salvador.

I was an oddity in Brazil. Most handicapped people in the villages of Central and South America don't go out in public. If they did, buildings and streets wouldn't be easily accessible to them anyway. A lot of the places we went I had to be piggy-backed in and my chair folded up and brought along because the doorways are very narrow and there are so many steps.

The people in wheelchairs that I did see were in hospitals. Many of them don't have the opportunity to have physical therapy, many of them have a lot of skin breakdowns because of the pressure sores that result from being in one position too long. Many of them look physically sick.

Kevin was asked over and over why I was in a wheelchair. It was always kind of funny, because even though I couldn't understand their language, I could tell I was being discussed by the way they looked at me out of the corners of their eyes!

I do live in a wheelchair. But my spirit and mind are not confined by it. I've never dreamed about my accident or about ending up in a wheelchair. I have had dreams that have wheelchairs in them. But in the dream, I'm never in the chair! Someone else is. For a moment after I wake up I wonder . . . , but then I realize it was a dream and I'm still paralyzed from the waist down.

Planning The Trip

I first tested the idea with Mom and Dad one night at the supper table. I had just come back from Brazil and Dad asked me what I was going to do next. "Go across the country in my wheelchair," I said, without giving it a lot of consideration.

Dad thought that was a little crazy, but he and Mom have seen us five guys through a lot of stuff, so I was pretty sure they were up to it if I was!

When I learned later that someone else had already crossed the lower forty-eight states in a wheelchair, I decided to start from Alaska and do something new. That was a sizeably larger bite since the route we took turned out to be 5600 miles rather than the coast-to-coast distance of 3200 miles.

Where did the idea come from? During high school my friends and I had often talked about hitchhiking or riding bike across the country. After the accident my old dreams often came back to me and I wondered if I could still accomplish them, but in a different way. My friends at Tabor asked, too, what I hoped to do after traveling to Brazil. They kind of laughed about it also, but I found responses like that made me a little more determined to try it!

Once my parents knew I was seriously thinking about the trip, they became concerned. They wondered if I was taking on too big a challenge, something I wouldn't get finished. And they worried that I could be hurt again. After all, this idea had echoes of the old cycle trip.

I began to get support for the idea from friends who were excited and encouraging. And as that grew, Mom and Dad decided that if I was really going to make the trip, they wouldn't be negative about it. Better yet, they started to support me! My whole family jumped in then, helping me train and helping get the trip lined up and organized.

I needed to prove to myself that I could reach a goal I set. It was my dream and I wanted to meet it for my own self-confidence and sense of self-worth.

But the longer this thing baked, the fuller it became. I had volunteered at some rehab hospitals and with youth groups during the summers. While I was in school I became part of a Big Brother program and worked at Rainbow's United Pre-school for handicapped children. Those people and their needs fused with my own during the months I stewed about the trip and finished up my senior year of college.

I was studying so I could professionally help the disabled. If, on my cross-country ride, I could benefit others who were also handicapped, and sensitize the able-bodied, I would multiply the good thing I first set out to do. That's when I thought of visiting handicap organizations and rehabilitation centers along the way, while raising funds for them at the same time.

By now this whole package was more than I could handle alone. Besides, I understood myself well enough to know that I needed people behind me just to make the trip. So I went to see my old high school friend, Myron Stoltzfus. We got to be buddies during our years at Lancaster Mennonite High School and we traveled together in Europe one summer. Myron has business experience and I wanted his help in organizing my dream. I came home from Kansas for my cousin's wedding in November, 1984. I visited Myron that weekend, almost two years after I first floated the idea before Dad and Mom at the supper table.

I took a letter along that evening, outlining, as clearly as I could for Myron's sake, how we might set things up. He got excited but asked for a month to think about whether he could meet my request—to not only organize the event, but to make contacts with people and places along the route I would travel, and to set up a nonprofit agency which could accept funds for handicap-related organizations and issue tax deductible receipts to donors.

When Myron and I checked in with each other in December, he had already talked with his lawyer, Doug Good, about the most advantageous way to set up our idea. Doug recommended that we form our own organization rather than work with an already established one. And that's where Hope for Life came from.

I had lived away from my home area for four and a half years, so Myron suggested and helped contact potential board members. We wanted people who would care about our cause, but who also had credibility in the community so folks would know this wasn't some Mickey Mouse deal. The idea of a reputable board of directors came from Myron's business head.

I had four people that I hoped would join the board—Myron, of course; Dr. Edwards P. Schwentker, my Hershey surgeon, whom I had long ago forgiven; Eileen M. Tymon, who oversaw my rehab at E-town; and Herman Glick, my pastor at Maple Grove Mennonite Church. Myron brought Doug Good, our attorney; Ike Stoltzfus, Myron's brother; and three local business persons, Francis I. duPont, Allon Lefever, and John S. Stoltzfus on board.

Things began to roll. Originally I assumed I'd make the trip during the summer of 1985, but time seemed short, and we began to look toward 1986 instead. Then plans fell together so well that summer 1985 again seemed possible.

Chris Slabaugh, a school friend of mine, Myron and I visited our local AAA, told them the cities and communities I wanted to hit, and they helped us map a route. A combination of reasons fed into my choice of stops. Five major cities were homes of the rehab centers I was raising funds for, and I definitely wanted to go through those places. So, for example, we went south to Denver and Colorado Springs and then back up to Elkhart, Indiana. Elkhart is a Mennonite community but it also has a rehab center I wanted to visit. Of course I wanted to get back to Edmonton and Calgary because of my emotional ties there. On the other hand, I chose not to go through Chicago because of time. I couldn't go everywhere!

Chris took AAA's general suggestions and began refining them by making phone calls into the areas to learn about road conditions. Later we made very few changes along the way, sticking basically to the route Chris finally proposed.

Myron researched how many miles I might be able to do in a day by checking with John Enright, the guy who had earlier wheeled across the States. He contacted some others who had run coast to coast for the Cancer Foundation to learn how they had generated interest in their fund-raising efforts. They sent us literature about how they organized their trip and their supporters.

We depended on our board of directors for financial and legal advice. But these people also became my friends. We were all new at this business and we had a kind of quiet first meeting! But in the four times we were all together before I left, the group became significantly helpful. And they became symbolic of the spreading enthusiasm that was gathering for the trip. In late April, just days before I flew to Fairbanks to start wheeling, some five hundred people gathered in Lancaster County for a send-off dinner, and my first fundraising event.

Meanwhile, I had been training. In early February I started putting in five miles a day and I couldn't believe how out of shape I was. It took me four hours to complete those first five miles. I came back the first day, worried I'd never make it.

I had been in weight training ever since my accident so I figured I had the strength for the trip, but I knew I had to build up my endurance. As time went on and I began to get into the rhythm, my conditioning improved. I got the five miles down to forty-five minutes, I began to add miles and stay out longer, and during the two weeks before I was to leave, I was doing fifty

Album Five: Calgary to Colorado

This was my fourth time back to Lake Louise since my accident in '78 (Banff National Park, Alberta); it was also the first time it was a beautiful sunny day while I was there.

Ranchester, Wyoming led us to a non-denominational church group which showed us some real Western hospitality.

(Below) Friends would join me at different times during the summer. Here Randy Witmer, (cousin) Dwight Stoltzfus and (brother) Kent flew to Montana to spend the weekend with me.

People would often stop and wonder what I was doing and would ask how to help. Thanks to this cyclist, the total contributions increased by $20.

As the heat increased, so did my water consumption (Douglas, Wyoming).

Denver, Colorado was an intermediate goal to reach this summer. *(Above)* Spalding Rehab put on a publicity rally for us. The Denver Broncos, the Nuggets and the Zephyrs were all represented there to greet me on my trip.

(Right top) I visited the children's hospital in Denver and was encouraged by their enthusiasm. They made a special poster for me.

(Right bottom) One of the many interviews that helped to increase publicity and awareness.

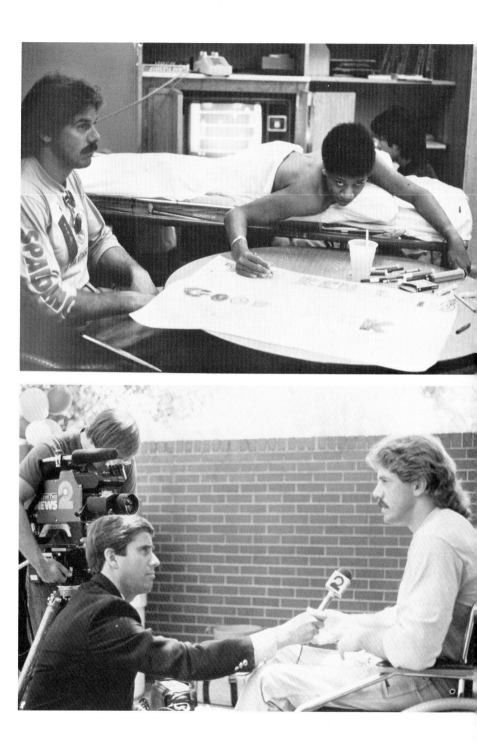

Colorado Springs made me leader of the pack when bicycles from the commu

ned me for the morning.

Back on the road, wondering what's next.

miles a day.

Then on April 22, my brother Curt and our cousin James Graybill left in the van for Fairbanks, Alaska. I flew from Philadelphia on the 26th and we all got into Fairbanks on Saturday morning, April 27. Don Shenk, a school friend who lives there, told us about a wheelchair race held annually in Anchorage. It was scheduled for Sunday morning, and I decided to join it. I was feeling pretty confident, but one small matter tripped me up! It was the spring weekend when the country switched to Daylight Savings Time. We all forgot to turn our clocks ahead when we went to bed, so I got to the race an hour late! I decided not to take our goof as a bad omen and went out and did the course anyway to see how good my time was. I didn't break any records!

I did pick up some tips from other racers. At their sugggestion I traded my hard-surfaced push rails for a set with more padding to save my fingers and hands, and with a finish that gave me better traction.

And I met Don Brandon, a wheelchair racer, living in Fairbanks. He told me he wished he could share his racing chair with me because it had twenty-inch front wheels rather than the eight-inch ones I had on mine. The bigger your wheels, the less friction you have, and the easier you roll down the road.

Only after I started did I learn that most cross-country racers have big front wheels. My chair worked well, however, for what I was doing. It was the only racer I had ever had, and I was used to it.

I wanted to roll! I was going to make it the whole way to Washington, D.C. and I hoped that along the way I would somehow give courage to handicapped people to find the determination within to get out and do something with their lives. I wished for them, too, all the support I was so graciously experiencing.

The Road Team and How They Made It Work

I knew from the beginning I couldn't do this job alone, so when I first talked to my friend Myron Stoltzfus about helping to make it work, I told him I needed at least two people in a van to follow me all the time.

As the plans firmed up, it became clear that I needed more than escorts. We needed help to publicize my coming into towns and cities so that fund-raising events could be set up, so that the media could be alerted and do their bit to promote the needs of the handicapped, and so that my speaking engagements and lodging could be arranged.

Myron's idea was to contact Messiah College near Harrisburg, Pennsylvania, to see if he could work out a summer intern program for students. They each got four hours of college credit for doing work in their fields of interest; I didn't need to worry about logistical details and could concentrate on pushing my chair! Steve Engle, a communications major, was out ahead of us two weeks. Part of his job was to drive the route we had mapped out ahead of time to see what the road conditions were like and to find out if there was any construction. If so, we would pick an alternate route. We did make some changes, but we never had to bypass any place that we wanted to go through. If someone said that another road was less traveled or had a better surface, we were flexible and changed our plans. But we never varied far from our original route.

Steve would often go to a town's police station or city hall and explain our work and ask whom he might see about a rally or a fund-raising dinner. Or he would check the listing of service clubs that often stand at the entrance to a town and then contact the local Jaycees or Lions Club. Sometimes he just wandered into a little local diner and started talking to people. He carried literature with him that explained all about our effort. Occasionally he'd contact motel chains and they would often offer us a night's free lodging! If we had a Mennonite church contact in the town or knew of a rehab hospital, he was always in touch with those folks, also.

Tim Haines, a business major, was the road manager. He, along with Lisa Wagner and Terri Shimer, would work the territory a day or two ahead of where I was. They were fine-tuning the work Steve had started.

They finalized our lodging, set up press conferences and interviews, took pictures, and told me what I'd need to do. Often I spoke or visited in hospitals, so I had to prepare for that as I pushed along during the day. Then each evening they'd drive back the fifty to seventy miles they had traveled out to be with us for the night.

On top of those four, who joined us in Edmonton, Alberta, there were always two guys in the van behind me. The van was for my physical safety, and the drivers kept me going! Because I moved slowly, usually in the driving lane, the van stayed twenty or thirty feet behind me with its flashers blinking. It had signs on it announcing "Hope for Life" and a map of our route across the continent.

Beginning in Fairbanks, Curt and James took turns driving since it gets kind of monotonous going so slowly, hour after hour. And often in the afternoons one of them would come out and ride bike with me to keep me company. We had brought along a beat-up old junker of a bike that we called Clyde.

Curt and James drove with me until Edmonton, Alberta. Then they flew home and two friends—Glenn Stoltzfus and Tim Raber—took over the van. Glenn came the rest of the way to Washington, D.C. with me. Tim was replaced by Lauren Martin in Denver, Colorado.

Originally we didn't know how important it would be to have front people ahead of us two weeks, and even two days. But we soon learned that mayors and governors and major ball teams need a little more lead time to prepare and clear their schedules.

The road team worked, and it paid off! For example, the governor of Colorado declared "Mike King Day" when I came into Denver. I met the Royals in Kansas City, and I sang the National Anthem when the Phillies met the Padres at Veterans Stadium!

Meanwhile, Myron was back home in Lancaster County, doing the accounting with the help of Diane Broujos, another Messiah College student. He worked hard to manage my schedule of speaking engagements and at drumming up publicity by phone. One of the difficulties for both Myron and me was that he would schedule me to be somewhere at a time that seemed reasonable from his end, but wasn't always possible from mine. Neither of us knew exactly what the other was going through, so we had to have a little give and take. And trust.

Of course none of us got paid. Not me, not Myron, none of the college students or my friends and family in the van. It was a volunteer summer for all of us.

On The Road

People don't expect to meet a wheelchair rolling down the Alaskan Highway. During my first week on the road folks drove toward me, their eyes bugging out of their heads, mouths wide open as they looked up over their dashes, wondering what was going on.

Our publicity machine had a limited audience in the Alaskan wilderness, so most everyone we met knew nothing about us. Again and again people would drive by, and a little while later they'd be back, wondering if they had seen what they thought they had, and curious about what I was doing.

Sometime during the first two weeks I met a bunch of truck drivers, and then we kept seeing those same guys over and over, making their runs. They had never seen anything like our little entourage and the more we saw them, the more questions they had for Curt and James on the CB radio. Naturally, they asked what was going on and, when we'd see them again, how I was doing.

Before we started, Cable News Network did a story about the trip and a few people early on had heard that. Some of them planned excursions up the Highway to look for us, and they'd always wish me luck.

I came into lots of small towns where the word spread quickly and people spilled out to watch. Now and then folks were actually looking and waiting for us, but more often they were shocked to see me coming down the Highway!

The morning we started out from the hotel and restaurant in Teslin, a little place in the Yukon Territory, a dump truck driver pulled up beside me, honked his horn, and looked at me like I was nuts. I headed on down the road, but I kept meeting him as he made his runs back and forth. Finally about noon he came by, stopped, and asked what I was doing. When I told him, he invited us into town that night. We had to drive back about forty miles, but there was no place on down the road anyway!

He took us to his home, cooked us moose steaks, potatoes, and some vegetables, and put us up there that night. He had gone to the Territory as an artist and he still goes out for a week at a time in the back woods to write and draw, but he drives a dump truck to earn a regular living. People like that, with their spontaneous help and warmth, I'll never forget.

Watson Lake is a big tourist and recreation center in the Yukon. When we got there, we saw some people we had met two weeks earlier, in White Horse, Yukon. They were expecting us, and had arranged our lodging and collected contributions for our meal costs! Later that evening they produced a little welcome celebration for us! So, the news of our trip was passed by word of mouth as well as by the media.

We ran alternately into surprise and recognition until we got to Edmonton, Alberta, where the population and, consequently, the press coverage, increased.

Because I didn't have speaking engagements in the evenings or hospitals to visit in those early weeks, we could take time to pull off and talk when people were curious. When we hit the open spaces again in Montana and Wyoming we'd stop and talk whenever we had the chance. But soon my schedule tightened up and I had to visit without losing sight of time. Covering the miles was a constant pressure.

At least half the 5605.8 miles I traveled, I was out on the road by myself. Curt and James took occasional afternoon rides on Clyde the bike, but mostly it was just me alone with the mountains.

Alaska was a real treat—aside from the difficulty of its terrain, of course! I ran with the mountains, so the snow-capped peaks kept me company on the south side, and once in a while on the north.

The trappers and hunters we met told bush and wildlife tales, among them stories about tree planters being mauled by bears. I saw only one bear and he took off for the woods when he spotted us. That was probably fortunate, although a little disappointing. Had I ever been in real danger because of a wild animal, I'd have been more worried. What I feared more was that somehow I wouldn't finish the trip.

Alaska was a good initiation the whole way around. I made my first visits to Boys' Clubs and Young Life Groups before I left Fairbanks. Then my high school friend, Don Shenk, organized a wheelchair race for the first fifteen miles of the trip, taking us to the town of North Pole. That's where I first tasted how strenuous this was going to be. I sized up the other guys and figured I could win, but I came in third! The Alaskan countryside was breathtaking and its people some of the most interesting I've met anywhere. Because their economy depends substantially on visitors, they are friendly and open about their lives. They invited us back to take us hunting and trapping. And I intend to go!

Dawson Creek was a major milestone. I had reached the end of the Alaskan Highway! We celebrated by taking off for the day. Ahead lay lots of speaking and visiting, in addition to miles of pushing.

Over the years I had led some Bible studies and discussion groups, and I took speech classes at Hesston College which helped me organize my thoughts and improve my delivery. I was a little shaky at first about how precise and sincere my message would sound. I thought and practiced a lot on the road, especially those days when I was scheduled to speak.

I didn't really have a chance to ease into the speaking routine. When we hit Edmonton, I spoke at two churches. Then, on each of the four nights between there and Calgary, I was in a different church, talking about living a fulfilled life, in spite of a physical handicap. By then the road crew had joined me, and I was grateful for their encouragement at those moments. I found it tough to put in a long day of road miles followed by speaking in the evening. When I didn't really feel like it, I had to reach deep inside and remind myself why I was out there, that this was what I wanted to do.

In Calgary I went back to Foothills Hospital where I had first been taken following my accident seven years earlier. Although they have only a small rehab department there, I was able to visit several patients. One was a guy with a recent spinal cord injury who wanted to know what physical therapy was like and what he should expect of the rest of his life, and whether he might ever again participate in sports events. He was a physical education teacher and he hoped to go back to that if he could. I encouraged him to try, and I relived a lot of my fears and frustrations seven years before. I had learned a lot, and now I had the chance to reflect on the helpful things in my recovery and point out ways other persons might better their skills.

I spoke and visited in nineteen hospitals along the way, concentrating on spinal cord injury centers, but including other organizations as well. The first was a Teen Center in Fairbanks, Alaska; Foothills Hospital in Calgary, Alberta; a group home in Conrad, Montana; a hospital in Casper, Wyoming; Spalding and Craig Rehab Centers and a childrens' hospital in Denver, Colorado; Frontiers Head Injury Center in Colorado Springs; an employment agency for the disabled in LaJunta, Colorado; Rainbows United in Wichita, Kansas; Bethany in Kansas City, Kansas; Arrowhead West, Inc. in Dodge City, Kansas; two in Missouri—Rusk Hospital in Columbia, and St. Johns Mercy Hospital in St. Louis; Loveway and MCC-DDS in Elkhart, Indiana; five in Pennsylvania—Hammelville Rehab in Pittsburgh, Hiram G. Andrews in Johnstown, Hershey Medical Center in Hershey, Elizabethtown Rehabilitation Center in E-town, Bryn Mawr Hospital in Bryn Mawr; Alfred

Album Six: Wichita to Kansas City

In Kansas, I could see grain elevators miles away. Sometimes I thought I'd never get there.

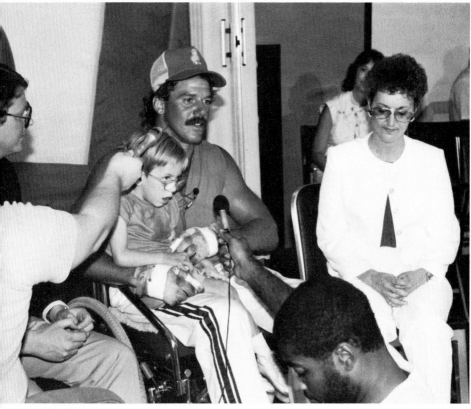

Wichita was a welcome sight.
(Above) Chris, a student at Rainbows United, got on camera with me. Rainbows United is where I did my social work placement through Tabor College. (Right top) Two of the Prairie Schooners joined me in wheeling into Newton where (right bottom) "Wheelchair Challenge Day" was proclaimed.

Kansas does have some hills. I guess that's where Hillsboro got its name.

n on my way to Tabor College in Hillsboro, Kansas.

Here I'm addressing the people of Hillsboro and thanking them for their support.

An elderly gentleman from the community, whom I had met many times during my years at Tabor, came to see me.

The cheerleading and basketball camp that invited me to stop in Emporia, Kansas. If I remember correctly, the one girl asked if I was married, and I answered "Not yet"!

Bethany Rehab of Kansas City, Kansas also welcomed us with a great publicity rally, beginning with a two-mile parade through the city.

I. duPont in Wilmington, Delaware; and National Hospital in Washington, D.C.

About one hundred patients and staff came to the gym at the Craig Rehab Center the Wednesday afternoon I was in Denver. Thanks to the area's many recreational facilities available for people in chairs, it was a healthy-looking bunch. They're taken on camping and river rafting trips and have access to a lot of modern equipment and wheelchairs. They were enthusiastic and curious. It was fun talking to a group who was knowledgeable about paraplegics' limitations.

Spalding Rehab held a fundraiser for us. In Colorado Springs a wheelchair basketball team rode through the city with me. I had occasionally played with a basketball team from Newton when I was in school in Kansas, so I really enjoyed those guys.

Bethany Rehab in Kansas City put together a parade that met me two miles away from the hospital and followed a route back to the center. Two members of the running club ran behind me carrying a banner. Some patients were pulled in a horse-drawn carriage. Several wheelchair athletes from the basketball and racing teams greeted us back at the hospital, along with the mayor and other representatives from the city. In all, between two and three hundred people gathered on the lawn to welcome us.

No doubt about it, I got excited. I found I could talk more clearly and easily about my goals and concerns with that kind of enthusiasm surrounding me!

When I went inside to visit with some patients who couldn't come out, they had another reception for me, this time complete with a birthday cake. What a day!

But it wasn't only in hospitals and rehab centers that I met handicapped people. I remember two blind people who showed up at one place. In Elkhart, Indiana, we visited some developmentally disabled and some Downs Syndrome children who built palates for a company and put nuts and bolts in bags. And I spent time with kids who have multiple sclerosis, cystic fibrosis, and muscular dystrophy. It was a summer of real exposure for me.

People had often told me I was an easy person to talk to. At school kids came up and talked a lot, and I realized then that because I was in a wheelchair they knew I wouldn't just take off and get away from them. Listening was one thing I could do to help other people, so I exercised in that way this summer, too. In fact, days that I didn't put on any road miles but had a lot of speaking and visiting engagements were more exhausting than the days I wheeled sixty miles.

There were those crazy times I tried both kinds of workouts. As we came toward Elkhart, Indiana, we were running a little behind schedule. I had wheeled as far as South Bend late that afternoon, but I wasn't going to make it into Elkhart for the evening where I was lined up to speak. So we packed up and drove in, then went back out to where I had stopped wheeling, and I put on some more miles, finally ending at one o'clock in the morning. That was the longest day I had.

I had the next day off, mileage-wise, but I had speaking engagements in four different places!

I noticed a funny thing. Personnel at rehab hospitals were usually more patient about my schedule than the church service planners, who were quite concerned that I be on time. But they didn't understand all the variables that could affect my day, compared to rehab center staffs who knew that weather and wind conditions could wreck the best laid schedule.

Chills, Hills, Gravel, and Rain

The worst road surface I pushed across was on the Alaskan Highway. When they built the road, they poured oil and then dumped crushed stone on top of that and let the traffic pack it down! The loose stuff eventually ended up on the edges, but the chips that remain in the traffic lanes are pretty big stones, compared to the chip-road surfaces in the States. It is far from smooth. Riding over that on wheelchair wheels is like being on a vibrator all day long! Towards the ends of those days the roughness had worn me out physically and mentally.

What's more, there are two hundred miles of gravel road on the Alaskan Highway. Most of it is packed down almost like a hard dirt surface and I could move fairly well on that. But the loose gravel was a different story, because it would catch my small front wheels and slow them up. Loose gravel on hills was worse yet. If it was steep I had to lean front so the chair wouldn't flip over, but if I leaned too hard, the backwheels would spin out. And then there were surprise holes and rocks that bounced me around a bit!

In fact I wore sunglasses sometimes to protect my eyes from flying stones. A couple of times stones came zooming by me from passing trucks and I thought that wearing a helmet might even be wise. But I didn't because I didn't want anything bulky on my head to make the wind resistance greater, or to cause me more discomfort.

Naturally, hills were the toughest terrain to get over. My average speed on a straightaway is ten miles an hour and on a downhill it's a lot faster, depending on the slope. I can move up a hill at five miles an hour, and that's a pretty good pace. But the real steep ones I travel at about two or three miles an hour.

Of course I had to lean front a little further on a steep grade so I wouldn't tip over backwards in the chair. Leaning over like that also gave me more strength and momentum to get a better push off the push rails.

It took determination and a lot of grunting to get up over some of those hills. Depending on how long and how steep they were, I would go for half a mile, stop for a minute to catch my breath and drink some water or eat a little, then go back to it.

The mountain that was the hardest to climb was on the Alaskan Highway. It was about three and a half miles from the foot to the top and it took me four hours to get up over it. Because it was all loose gravel, I had to find the right way to lean to keep from spinning or somersaulting backward.

The longest slope I had was a thirty-mile one and that one took me six hours to get over. Fortunately, it wasn't as steep nor as rough a road surface as the previous one on the Alaskan Highway!

Sometimes people coming toward me from the opposite direction would greet me with the news, "Oh, man, you're going to have a rough day tomorrow. A lot of hills ahead!" I learned not to let that get me down because usually they hadn't assessed things right. They simply didn't realize what was hard and what was manageable for me. In fact, often they would assure me of "only a few short hills ahead," when, in fact, they were hard climbs because they were so steep!

From Fairbanks to Denver, the road team gave me a report each day about how many hills I was going to have and what kinds of road surfaces to expect. Then from Denver to eastern Pennsylvania, I preferred to discover the road conditions when I got there since that was territory I was more familiar with. But there were still surprises.

Coming into Harrisburg, Pennsylvania we heard there was a detour around some major road work. We sent Tim ten miles on ahead to see what was going on and to find out if we could get through or if we'd have to pick another route. The detour was twenty-eight miles further than the original road would have been, and that twenty-eight miles would have really thrown off my time schedule that day. Tim talked to the guys who were working on the bridge, and they let us all go through, even though the road was closed to other traffic.

They could have been nasty but they caught the spirit of what I was doing and wanted to help me in the best way they could. People everywhere really worked with us!

Even when I slowed traffic considerably by traveling in the main lane, people seldom got upset. If there was a good shoulder I'd use it, but most of the secondary roads had uneven edges or loose gravel along the sides and weren't in safe or good shape.

There was three feet of snow on the ground when we left Fairbanks, Alaska, on the afternoon of April 30, but all the roads were cleared. The skies were blue, the weather was beautiful. As we neared the tops of hills we had some snow showers coming off the passes, but coming down the other side we rolled out of the clouds into sunshine. The roadway was wet, but it was only coming down Beaver Creek Pass that a couple inches of snow collected on the road.

I expected much rougher weather the whole way along. In the spring a snowstorm can suddenly move through the mountains, but we escaped! In fact we had no rain until Trutch Mountain in northeastern British Columbia, near the end of the Alaskan High-way. Then it rained for two solid days. After that we had sunny skies again until we got to Calgary, Alberta where we ran into thundershowers.

Our next real downpour wasn't until Missouri when we had to go through a full day of rain. Then we had a lot of thundershowers from Missouri all the way into Ohio.

The rains had little effect on me and the road surfaces. But they did cause a bit of a problem on the push rails, those little inner wheels that I push to make the chair go. My leather gloves got wet and, consequently, slippery. Normally I didn't have to grab hold of the push rails very tightly because they are foam-covered and kind of sticky, so I would just hit against them. But when it rained and they got wet, I had to grab ahold of them as well as push. It made the going a little slower and tougher.

At the beginning of the trip we had freezing temperatures during the Alaskan mornings. But during the day, it warmed up to forty-five or fifty degrees.

The four days before we reached Wichita, Kansas, temperatures drifted between one hundred and one hundred five degrees. But that wasn't too bad because the humidity wasn't sky-high. In fact, Missouri and Illinois were really wearing because of their peak humidity. Even Pennsylvania, known for its mugginess, offered us bearable humidity. I think we picked one of the nicest summers in memory, weather-wise.

Mixing Up The Monotony

Every morning before we started, we set the meter on the van to count that day's miles. Watching the miles add up is reward enough for a while. But I needed a few additional incentives to keep myself going.

So we dropped in on some major league ball clubs along the way. Farm boys growing up in rural Pennsylvania imagine that their sports heroes are eight feet tall and super human! But when Dan Reeves of the Denver Broncos shook my hand, I sensed he was a normal person. He came to me after a welcoming ceremony, and in a very relaxed way, visited for a while. His manner was so easy he felt like a friend whom I'd known for a long time. Both he and the representative from the Nuggets, Denver's basketball team, invited me to give them a call when I'm back in town so I can be their guest at a game. I'm eager to try, to see if they do remember me and their promises! Experiencing the personal side of these people was a real bonus.

Willie Williams of the Kansas City Royals took us down to their club house and introduced us to a number of the players, among them George Brett, whom I've followed. These guys joked around and had a good time, too, and once again I was struck with how human they are.

The St. Louis Steamers invited me back to watch them play soccer on their indoor field. And in St. Louis we also met some of the Cardinals—Darryl Porter, Ozzie Smith, Whitey Herzog, and Tommy Herr, whose home isn't very far from mine in eastern Pennsylvania. They were comfortable to be around, and seemed genuinely interested in what I was doing.

The Cards played the Phils the night we were in St. Louis. Later back at the hotel I was introduced to Von Hayes, the Philadelphia Phillies' center fielder. We talked a while and I explained my trip. I saw him again when I got into Philadelphia, and he came up to me and said, "Hey, I remember you from St. Louis. Did it really take you three weeks to get in here?"

I couldn't have hoped for more honest affirmation than I got from these guys. I felt like they were responding as athletes to another athlete. They gave me as much recognition as I've seen them receive as superstars. I was touched by their human sides.

One idea we had early on was to see if I could be scheduled to sing the National Anthem at one of the ball games we attended along the way. We worked at lining it up while we were on the trip but learned, as I was coming toward Kansas City, that it wasn't going to be possible at any of the parks, so I stopped practicing and worrying about it.

But Monday afternoon as we rolled toward Philadelphia, I was told I was slated to sing. That night. At the Phillies game. Okay, I thought, at least I have no time to get nervous!

I am a part of a church that has not participated actively in government or the military, and I don't consider myself a highly patriotic person. But I respect our country, and so I didn't feel it was a conflict for me or my family if I sang that night. In fact, it was a pretty high moment. Being down on the field, being so near

Album Seven: Ozarks to Appalachians

Missouri and the Ozarks brought heat, humidity and rain. This day was full of fixing flats; we had five that day.

Food was important to keep me going. Between breaks they would feed me as we moved along!

St. Johns Mercy Hospital in St. Louis greeted me with members from the St. Louis Steamers indoor soccer team and three of their cheerleaders. Here I am being presented with a jersey from the Steamers.

Visiting the locker room of the Cardinals was a highlight also. I met a number of the players and especially enjoyed meeting Tommy Herr (his home is near mine).

Crossing the Mississippi River over one of the older bridges. Onward to Illinois.

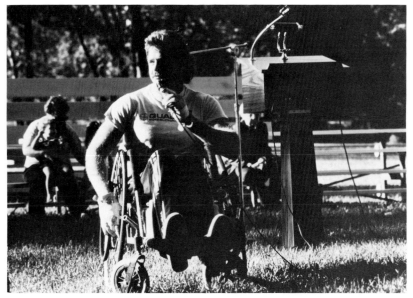

(Above) A bit behind schedule, we drove to Elkhart, Indiana to keep the schedule for their rally.

(Below) We made up those miles that evening, finishing in Elkhart at 1:00 a.m. I had to read the map by the lights of the van.

(Left, top) From Fort Wayne, Indiana to the Ohio line, we were escorted by the Sheriff's Department. (Left, bottom) Hesston College friend Jim Schlabach joined me for two days near Holmes County, Ohio. (Above) The last mountain of the Appalachian Range (Tuscarora); it was a tough one.

Although I didn't talk much, riding companions were nice. Here Kerry Stutzman is pictured with me. She joined me in Akron, Ohio, and completed the trip with me.

the players, meeting several of them, and then watching the game at close range was a dream come true. I got through the song without any problems, and then they had a ceremony for me at home plate, recognizing my efforts for the handicapped. I'd list that evening among the highlights of my trip!

I had my best days when I met surprising people. We came into one small Kansas town and a little girl and her grandma were waiting for me. She came up and asked, "Why in the world would you ever want to do anything like this, especially at this time of year?" It was one hundred four degrees that day, and I knew she meant her question sincerely. I told her about my trip and why I was wheeling and she said, "Boy, I'd rather be swimming!" Children were fun to talk to because they said whatever was on their mind.

In Ranchester, Wyoming, a bunch of little kids wanted to come out and ride bike with me. They were curious about my chair and how it worked.

When I'd speak in a church and bring my racer along in so the audience could see what I traveled in, it was the kids who would play around and ride in it. Usually if they were five and under they'd come up, feel the wheels, grab ahold of the thing, and push it around to see how it moves. Often I'd be sitting, talking to a group of adults, and I'd feel myself rocking around and rolling a bit. I'd look down and there would be a child checking out the chair and feeling it. I think most kids are fascinated by anything that has wheels on it.

A boy in a wheelchair rode through the town of Roundup, Montana with me. I felt like I really encouraged him and became a kind of hero to him. I gave him a real thrill when I grabbed hold of his chair as we went down a hill. His chair had no steering capacity, but by holding onto it, I was able to steer it along with mine.

Emporia, Kansas was a real kicker! As we came into town the heat was oppressive and I was feeling kind of down because I was running behind schedule. What I didn't know was that a basketball camp and cheerleading camp were being held for high school kids at the Emporia State University. The kids heard I was coming through town and asked their coaches if they could invite me to the campus.

Meanwhile, we had already wheeled through the town and were seven miles beyond it before anyone realized that I had been there and gone. So they sent the Campus Police out to catch us and ask if we'd come back in. I was worried about how late I'd have to run that night, but I wondered who wanted to meet us. When he said, "Six hundred cheerleaders," I said, "I'll follow you!" And we turned around.

It was wild because the town had seemed empty, and suddenly I was surrounded by a thousand people! I spent between thirty and forty-five enthusiastic minutes out on a parking lot with them. The cheerleaders had prepared cheers that morning; the four hundred basketball guys came out, chanting phrases they were taught in camp to keep their spirits up.

Their statement for the week was "Yes, I can," and they gave me a T-shirt and stickers with the slogan on. Then suddenly they were gone and I went back to the quietness of the road, glad I hadn't missed those thousand kids and their well-timed good wishes.

From there all the way home, the memory of the chant kept me company, especially during the hard times.

Nasty response was minimal. The first I remember was on the road coming into Garden City, Kansas, where a section was under construction. A lot of traffic had backed up behind us and some guy in a pick-up roared out around us, hollering, "Get off the road."

A similar thing happened once or twice in Missouri. Both times there was no shoulder and there were only two lanes, so we were right out on the road. It was hard for traffic to get around us quickly because we stretched out considerably. While going through towns or more heavily populated areas, we usually had a police escort in the lead. I followed them, with the bikers and van behind all of us.

We seldom varied from the route we had originally planned. There were a few detours that made us travel some extra miles but most of the time construction workers let me and the road crew go right through where they were working.

And nearly every place we visited was directly on our route. If we had to make an appearance off our track, we just loaded up everybody, drove in to the place, then came back to where I had stopped wheeling, to start again.

I seldom worried about travel details unless I wanted to. The road crew set things up, but checked with me to see if it was possible to be "here" at this time and then "there" two hours later. They depended on me to gauge my travel time; I counted on them to tell me what was coming up and what I needed to prepare for. I liked to know about my speaking commitments about two days out so I could gear myself up.

My record day, distance-wise, was eighty miles, coming into Wichita, Kansas. I had done seventy miles on the day from Dawson Creek to Grand Prairie in Alberta, Canada. Those were good times because of easy ups and downs, hills gradual enough that I could nicely mount them, and then downhill stretches that I could coast on, giving myself a little break. The weather was pleasant and there were people biking with me and wishing me well along the road. I never got tired of hearing that encouragement, over and over.

People in Montana and Wyoming and those more thinly settled areas were particularly friendly, taking us into their homes, telling us about their country. And yet we found those kinds of folks everywhere.

The hardest days were those when I didn't feel well physically. Sometimes I got behind in sleep or I was worn out by the demands I was making on my body and spirit. I fought blisters on my hands, especially on the lower half of my thumbs and in my palms. Going up hills meant that I needed to grab the push rails with strength on that part of my hands. If I was on flatlands I moved the pressure point to the upper part of my index fingers and the very base of my thumbs.

I treated the sore spots with salve, and someone helped me tape my fingers every morning before I put on gloves. That protected my skin and helped keep my hands dry. In the end, I wore out fourteen pairs of leather gloves. My hands were swollen most of the summer, especially the knuckles on my thumbs and index fingers and I believe my fingers are a little more crooked now than before my trip.

I worked hard and I ate lots. And I quickly saw the direct relationship between eating the right kind of food and having enough strength to get through the day. A lot of churches generously fed us, but sloppy joes and hamburgers lack something in nourishment when you exert yourself as much as I did each day. Once we had hamburgers three nights in a row and by the fourth day I could feel that my energy was way down. I made it through the day, but it was rough and slow. No one was trying to skimp on us; I was just on a strenuous marathon.

I concentrated on protein and carbohydrates or high calorie foods—potatoes, pasta, pizza and a lot of cereal in the mornings. I snacked on trail bars and ate fruit regularly.

Often on the way up a hill, I'd be moving along slowly and the guys would come out, run along beside me, and feed me a banana or an orange. They'd just kind of reach over and put it in my mouth and I'd take a bite. Lauren would sometimes ride up beside me on his bike, and because he was trying not to run into me, sort of smear the fruit around on my face trying to get it into my mouth! Normally we stopped for a fifteen- to twenty-minute lunch, and took another ten-minute break during the afternoon.

I put away barrels of water. In the north, when we first started, we filled the five-gallon water jug every second or third day. But as the temperatures warmed up, we filled it daily and, occasionally, more than once a day. One really hot and humid day in Missouri I used five gallons of water. I drank three gallons and the other two got dumped over me!

I seldom drank sodas because they simply couldn't replenish my body fluids as they needed to be when I was working that hard. Water is best at that, and it's cheaper, too.

I learned I am a people person. Days got long faster and I tired more quickly when we were in the middle of nowhere without people around. It's not that I mind being alone. In fact, there were days when I wished for a little more privacy, but I depended a lot on hearing support from the sides of the roads. And I rate as high points those places where I met school friends and worked with patients in rehab centers.

Mornings passed quickly. I was fresh and raring to go, and usually banged out twenty-five to thirty miles before lunch. But the distance between thirty and forty miles seemed to take forever. Once I got past forty, though, I caught my second wind and was ready to knock off the last ten, fifteen or twenty miles. That final stretch went pretty fast.

Often one of the road crew came out and rode bike with me during the afternoons. Time moved faster and I stopped thinking about how tired I felt when I had someone to talk to and carry on with. And I listened to a lot of music, now and then singing along, sometimes practicing the National Anthem, just in case!

Imitating Scooby Doo, Bert and Ernie, Donald Duck, Sylvester, and Porky Pig got me over all kinds of hills and through all sorts of sticky heat. Now and then passersby gave me strange looks, but I knew I was harmless even if they weren't sure!

When I didn't have an obligation, I tried to really relax in the evenings. About half the nights we stayed in homes and the rest of the time in hotels. Instead of worrying or getting all steamed up for the next day, I'd watch TV and unwind, visit a little or go out to a movie.

I tried to get to bed by ten o'clock, but that wasn't always easy, especially in the north because the sun was still high at that hour. But during the hottest parts of the summer we were often rolling by six in the morning to beat the heat, so I had to turn in the night before in decent time.

When we reached the Pennsylvania state line we began to feel home country! We stopped there for awhile, whooped, hollered, and screamed at each other. Then we dutifully got back to business. Ahead of us lay some of the worst humidity yet, one of the toughest mountains I had to face (in the Tuscarora Range), and a near accident that could have overshadowed the whole adventure.

The road crew and I were a kind of curious-looking outfit as we moved along the highways, and I often noticed people turning around, looking at me after they had passed, trying to figure us out. What I could see before they did was that they were not yet back in their lane—and traffic was coming on. They'd quickly swerve and I'd give thanks that we had avoided an accident.

On the day we left Johnstown, Pennsylvania, we were coming down off a mountain onto a highway that was widening from two lanes into four. A lot of traffic that had been backed up was coming around us in a steady line. I was in the far right lane when a guy came up on us, unaware of how slowly we were moving, despite the fact that our van's warning lights were blinking. He suddenly saw he was right on top of us, locked up his brakes, but still plowed into the rear of the van. The skid marks were about twenty-five feet long.

Normally Glenn drove the van twenty or thirty feet behind us, but he was within ten or fifteen feet of me at that moment because we were on a slope out of the mountain. He saw the car approaching and was able to turn off the road onto the shoulder as soon as he was hit. Otherwise the van would have run right over the two bikers and me since the impact shoved it forward.

The driver of the car was pretty shaken and his vehicle was fairly heavily damaged. Our van escaped with only some minor scrapes.

There were those special days when I counted hard on my adrenalin. I was running on five-hour nights of sleep when I rolled into Hershey Medical Center on August 22, intent on not being late, ready to celebrate not only my trip, but also the completeness of my recovery which began in earnest at that place. From there we went to Elizabethtown Rehab Center for an emotional gathering with people who had encouraged me back to life, then on to Lancaster with a growing stream of bicyclists, many of whom were my friends.

The West Fallowfield Christian School, where I had gone for my elementary years, was the site of a welcome beyond belief. Two thousand people came to eat barbecued chicken, hear me speak and accept our local Congressman's suggestion that the next space shuttle be equipped for a handicapped person, with me as a candidate for the slot!

I slept at home that night, totally exhausted. The next morning I spoke at Maple Grove Church, and in the afternoon Grandma Zook cooked us a wonderful dinner. I was at home, and I was happy, but I had three more days to push to finish the trip. So that Sunday night I went out and put on twenty miles.

I rolled up to the Capitol Building steps in Washington, D.C. on August 28, one hundred twenty days and 5,605.8 miles after leaving Fairbanks, Alaska. White House representative Bob Sweet, who acts as an advocate for the disabled, and Congressional and city dignitaries all welcomed me.

But the faces in the crowd I best remember were those who had invested energy, dollars, time, and hope in my life, at those moments when I could never have gone on, had I been alone—

Mom and Dad, my brothers, the Hope for Life board members, the road crew, my friends. They had sustained me, and so had my faith.

If We Were Doing It Again

We fought a constant tension on the road—to keep our schedule, mileage-wise, and yet to be relaxed enough to meet people at a satisfying depth.

The two-pronged effort was at the core of my adventure, and it provided the energy that kept me going—to cover the country in my wheelchair, and to visit with and speak for the handicapped whenever I could. But I felt pulled between the two most of the way.

If I were starting now from scratch, I'd certainly do both again, but I would somehow try to add more time.

Had we taken several more months to plan the trip, we may have received more publicity nationally. That would probably

Album Eight: Home to Pennsylvania

Former coordinator of E-town Hospital, Eileen Tymon, good friend and medical consultant, congratulates me at E-town. If I had a dollar for all the hugs I got from her, I'd be rich!

Invited to Dickinson College, I was greeted by the football squad (above). I also met Pete Johnson, an attorney who missed me in Lewistown and drove to Carlisle to see me (below).

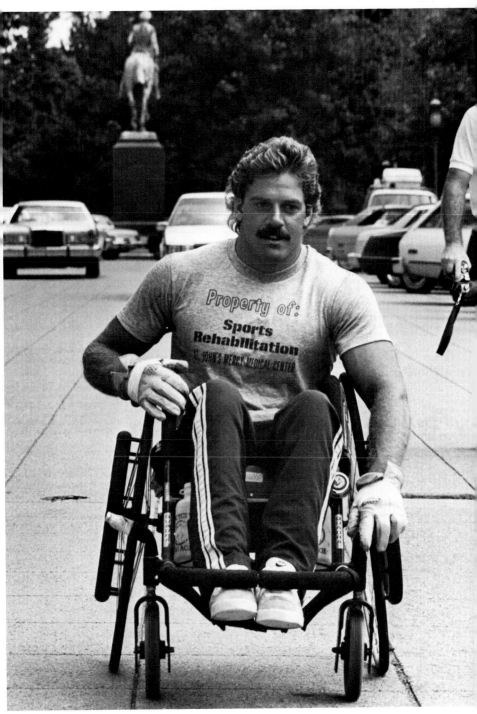

I finally reached Harrisburg, our state capital.

Family members came to meet me individually all along the way this summer. It happened again here at Hershey Medical Center.

E-town Hospital is where I got my start in '78. Seeing this welcome showed me that they continue to give people the start they need.

(Right, top) Eileen giving thanks, recognition and welcome to those who joined the ceremony.

(Right, bottom) Michael Horst congratulates me. Mike was at E-town during the fall of '78 when I was.

Getting back to Lancaster Square!

'ith 5500 miles behind me, I reached West Fallowfield School in my home commu

The whole day was filled with excitement and people (left). Bikers were with me all day. (Above) Congressman Bob Walker congratulates me and promises to recommend me for the Space Shuttle!

Grandpa King enjoyed the festivities.

It was great that the largest crowd this whole summer was in my home whole way.

nity. After all, it was they who encouraged me and supported me the

My adorable cousin Noreen.

have generated increased awareness about handicap concerns, yet people's attention spans are pretty short anyway. And they're more likely to be touched by *seeing* someone working in a wheelchair than by hearing it's *going* to happen.

Longer-range planning may have resulted in more fund-raising events sponsored by rehab hospitals, handicap organizations and service and community clubs. And we may have enlisted the endorsements of more celebrities, dignitaries, and sports stars. But then I may have been tempted to overlook the less attractive people in wheelchairs, for whom I was making this trip anyway.

Maybe we should have waited another year to go, but our juices were up and we decided to roll before we got entangled by more "reasonable" obligations.

Furthermore we were all volunteers. Having a larger advance crew, spreading enthusiasm among Lions and Kiwanis Clubs and Jaycees several months ahead of our coming, may have paid off in more funds for Hope for Life. And we could likely have swelled the numbers of people willing to walk through towns with me or "Bike-with-Mike," had we hit more major cities. (Bikers and walkers found sponsors to pay a certain amount of money for each mile they traveled with me, to be donated to Hope for Life.)

But a team of that size and on that kind of schedule would have needed significant financial support. And they would have worked so far ahead of the event, we likely would have sacrificed the zest that our gang had. We were driven by immediacy and personal commitment to the effort.

Most of all, I wish I could have spent more time with people along the roads and with patients in rehab centers and hospitals. I don't remember that we ever turned anyone away who had questions or wanted to talk, but I sometimes felt we were a little clipped because I had to keep moving. We handed out a lot of brochures about the project, and asked people to read them for a fuller explanation.

I was frustrated in hospitals where I'd breeze in, give a speech, then move out so I could get on to the next place. I'd leave behind people who wanted to talk personally. I guess that's the way those kinds of events have to run in order to contact as many people as possible.

Had I slowed my schedule too drastically, my physical endurance may have slacked. I needed to take rest days and more slowly paced days, but too many back to back would have hurt my strength more than helped it.

I didn't train as much as I should have before beginning the journey. When I started in Alaska I was averaging only five miles an hour. When I finished the trip I was doing ten miles an hour. And I was ready to re-do that race out of Fairbanks. I think I could win on a second try, or at least give the winner more competition!

Without Hope for Life, the board, and the road crew, little of substance would have happened. I would change nothing fundamental about any of our organization, except to improve some communication and scheduling difficulties. But those wrinkles seem inevitable, given the geographical distance at which we were working, and the number of groups to which Hope for Life was channeling funds.

I owe many people thanks for their gifts to the handicap organizations we were financially supporting—from the corporate donors, to the children who handed me coins, to the hitchhiker who flagged me down, asked what I was doing, then fished out a twenty-dollar bill. Those moments were priceless. I wouldn't change them for anything. They will warm my memory for a long time.

I Learned A Lot

I've become an expert on road surfaces, I've learned plenty about how humans who are curious behave. I've seen more open sky in four months than in the first twenty-six years of my life. But I've probably learned more about myself than anything else during my wheelchair tour.

I pushed at the limits of my physical capacity. I've tested my determination. And I want to commit the strength I found within to making the lives of handicapped people more fulfilling.

As I trained and then as I pushed, I told myself I was on a summer-long marathon race. I ran cross-country in high school, but this journey required training to build endurance. Keeping my strength became critical, so I learned to discipline my eating and sleeping in order to go day after day. In fact, I found that resuming after a three-day break, which I took in Alberta to visit friends, was a tough fight for my body and my will. If I had ever lost my conviction about doing this thing to the end, I would not have finished.

I came to believe more in people. I did not expect the volume of good response we received, often from folks whom I met only briefly. I know now that there are people scattered everywhere who care about others. I take a lot of comfort in knowing that if I need help, I'm likely to find someone who will offer it.

The thing I feel most successful about was showing what people in wheelchairs are capable of doing—if they are determined and have the right people supporting them.

Able-bodied folks thanked me for pointing out what ought to be done to better accommodate the disabled. The handicapped along the way seemed pleased that I was addressing the need to better equip our society for people in wheelchairs.

It wasn't always easy for me to talk with the severely handicapped. I was nervous, especially at first, when persons with great speech difficulties because of head injuries came to talk with me. I couldn't always understand them and I was afraid of humiliating them because they wanted so intently to be heard. Toward the end of the trip I became better able to grasp what they were saying. And, consequently, I lost most of my nervousness.

Those encounters always made me grateful for what I do have—a good mind and a strong upper body so that I get around well, compared to people who need someone else's assistance all the time.

Nor was it easy to visit with folks who were recently disabled. Sometimes I met patients whose feelings resembled my own during therapy—somebody in a wheelchair was the last person I wanted to see then. When I sensed that, I didn't stick around long. I didn't want to pry into their business or make them talk. No one was hostile, but a few times things were tense because people were struggling with the initial shock of their injuries. I remember well those days in my own recovery.

My training to become a social worker for the handicapped began in a nitty-gritty way on the trip. And I came face-to-face with the sometimes terrible, sometimes hopeful truth that all of us have a disability of some kind to live with.

One bonus from the summer is the racing tips I picked up. The best place to hit the push rails is just past the top of the wheel on the front where it starts curving down. If you start below the top, on the back of the wheel, you actually resist the flow that you already have going. Pacing is important, of course, including the number of times you push yourself. I learned that if I pushed constantly, I got quickly fatigued without giving myself any more speed.

And I found I enjoyed ceremonies and recognition, yet I was always a little frightened by the fuss. The first time I heard that a state might proclaim a "Mike King Day" was in Colorado. I was kind of embarrassed and felt like I didn't really deserve that. At the same time I was warmed to realize that state officials were supportive of my effort and wanted to give it wider notice. It was an idea that caught on rather broadly—Colorado, Kansas, Missouri, Indiana, Ohio, and Maryland each designated a "Mike King Day."

But my home state of Pennsylvania helped me keep my feet on the ground by deciding against doing it! I guess Governor Thornburgh didn't want to start a precedent of setting aside a special day for just any near-hero.

Everything You Ever Wanted to Know About Wheelchairs

I didn't know a thing about wheelchairs until I needed one.

Now I use three different kinds and they are the three basic models made—a standard chair that weighs about fifty pounds; a sports model, used for basketball, tennis, and racquetball; and a lightweight racing chair for anything from sprints to marathons. The sports model and racer both weigh about twenty-two pounds.

Wheelchairs are custom-made. You're measured so your chair fits you. Then you can choose not only the style you want but also the kind of padding and cushions that best fit your needs.

My standard chair costs $800. It's handy, but not very good for sporting events. The sports model goes for about $1800 and the racing chair I used on the trip costs about $1400.

That chair was a standard racer that the Quadra Chair Company in California gave to me for the trip—and to keep. It was their way of helping to sponsor me.

The company has made this particular kind of chair for seven years, especially for wheelchair Olympics.

I had the same frame for the whole trip. But we had to replace both the front and the back wheels numerous times, as well as the front casters that hold the front wheels in the frame. The thing took a real beating, withstanding all kinds of road conditions, but it still held up. We had a spare frame along in case the original one broke.

If I were going out on the road again I would choose larger front wheels than the eight-inch high ones I used. I would want at least twenty-inch wheels so that the friction would be less and I could go faster. And I'd probably select push grips of various sizes. They are those center wheels that you actually push to make the chair go. The littler ones give you more speed and the bigger ones more torque or power. They are made as small as twelve inches in diameter or as large as eighteen inches. I used two sizes—fifteen-inch ones from Fairbanks to Pueblo, Colorado, and fourteen-inch ones from there on.

Crown compensators would have helped adjust my front wheels on roads that were higher in the center than along the edges. Crowned roads always made me push especially hard with my right arm.

It is possible to adjust your seat up and down. That really depends on the length of your arms and how high you'd like to be from the wheels or how low you want to sit into them.

On sports and racing chairs, the wheels are bowed out at the bottom to give you a wider wheel base and, consequently, a wider balance so you don't tip over as easily. And that angle also keeps the tops of the wheels in closer to your upper body so you don't scrape your arms on the wheels.

I would often get black marks on my inner arms between my elbows and shoulders. But if the wheels had stuck out further, I'd have had some pretty mean brushburns.

A sports model has a wide black shield around the inner edge of its wheels which serves as a spokeguard. If someone runs into you or a ball slams the wheel, it won't break the spokes as easily as if the chair didn't have one.

I like my sports chair. It scoots around a little more easily than my standard one because it's lighter. And it looks a little sharper.

None of my chairs have brakes which I could use to slow myself on a downhill, although it is possible to get them if I'd want. (The chairs do have "parking" brakes that keep me from drifting if I'm sitting on an incline.) Coming down slopes I would just hang on to the front wheels to guide myself, and to take the edge off my speed. I'd crouch down in a tuck position so that my chest was lying flat on my knees. That certainly helped the aero-dynamics. It shifted a little more weight to the front wheels, but not enough to tip me forward. The wide wheelbase prevented that.

A trucker clocked me coming down the highest point on the Alaskan Highway at seventy miles an hour. That was my fastest speed. Normally, I'd get up to forty-five or fifty miles an hour coming down a hill, depending on how steep and long it was. I'm glad I didn't know how fast I was going till I got to the bottom that time!

As far as controlling the chair, the steering wheels are the front wheels. They keep it going in a straight line or guide it around turns. Naturally you can't make any sharp turns going that fast, but I usually let the chair do whatever it would do. When it came to controlling the speed, I could brake by just rubbing my hand against the wheel. I couldn't make a real fast stop, but I could slow myself down and eventually stop if I had to. And I didn't hurt my hands because of all the padding and gloves I wore.

The van always preceded me coming down mountains. They gave me one of the two-way radios and kept the other themselves so they could tell me what was ahead. Twice, coming out of Steamboat Mountain in British Columbia, we thought we were down and the van came around behind me. We had plateaued, but suddenly there was a steep slope on a curve and I couldn't hold the chair in my lane. Thank God, there were no cars coming, because I could have done nothing to protect myself. None of us had ever been on that highway before and there was no way we could have calculated either the angles of the curves or the steep-ness of the road.

Album Nine: The Final Stretch

The final leg of my trip led me to the DuPont Rehab Center in Wilmington, Delaware.

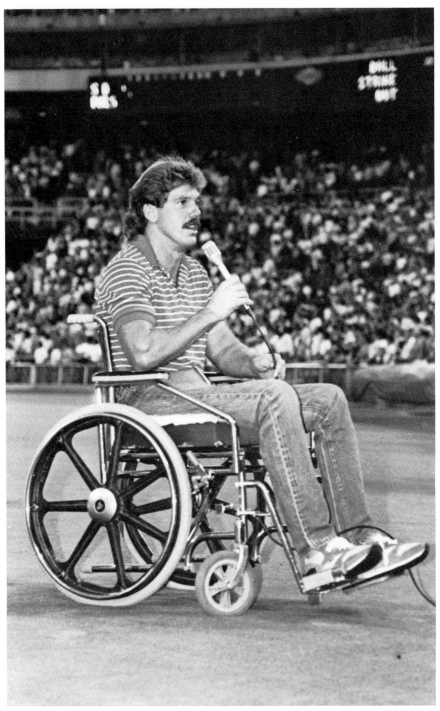

Singing the National Anthem was a moment I'll always remember.

The Phillies game where I received a presentation from John Felske (manager), and talked with the players (Glen Wilson).

Hard to believe it, my goal is in sight.
A wonderful welcome as I complete my challenge.

Question and answer time. (Below) The road crew (missing is Lisa Wagner & Terry Shimer).

My very supportive family.

Well, on with my life! As this book goes to press, I'm beginning my Master's program in social work at the University of Pennsylvania.

The Rest of My Life

My disability has simply become part of the way I live. When I get up in the morning, I lift myself out of bed and into my chair. The only time I really think about my handicap is when I meet a limitation, like not being able to reach something out in the shop at home, or coming upon a step when I'm trying to go somewhere.

I'm bothered about it, too, when I watch my three favorite sports—water skiing, snow skiing, and ice hockey. I know I can't play them, at least in the way I did before. But I may figure out a new way to manage them. I keep finding different and easier methods of getting things done.

One thing I'm not used to is being recognized when I go out

somewhere! I still feel like the same person I was before I made my cross-country trip. And I'm ready to be ordinary again. I hope the people who peeked around the corner at me while I was at the bank this morning remember why I wheeled across the country.

I'll be feeling the call of the road from now on, I'm sure. And I intend to stay in shape so I can keep participating in marathons. But I have a new challenge now. I'm studying for a master's degree in social work so I can have the job I want.

I had wonderful care when I was a patient at Elizabethtown Rehabilitation Center. But there was a major gap in my therapy. I had no one to talk to who really understood what I was going through and who could have provided some counseling for me. It was hard for me to just go up to someone and begin talking, but if someone had asked me questions, I would have been able to respond.

I had the physical part of my therapy together when I left E-town, but I needed a person to talk to who had experience with what I was going through, either personally, or by working closely with others who did. That's the service I want to offer in a rehab program. I'd skip getting the degree if I could, since I feel like the accident, my recovery, and my time as a volunteer and visitor in hospitals all qualify me pretty well. But I'll gain some helpful techniques in classes and in my field work, so my time isn't wasted.

And depending on street conditions and the distance between my apartment and the University of Pennsylvania's School of Social Work, I'll use my racer in Philadelphia, so I don't lose the feel of the road.

I don't expect to leave school equipped with a lot of profound things to say to people lying in beds or training in a rehab center. Because when I reflect on my experience, it wasn't what folks said to me that began to help me heal. It was just their being with me when I needed them.

And I have experienced that in reverse. A lot of times when I visit people in hospitals I say almost nothing. But they talk because they need someone to listen. I'm learning ways I can help patients begin airing their feelings if they want to, and that requires no great wisdom on my part. I just try to give bits of encouragement and support when I get the chance.

My grandparents and my aunts and uncles tease me that by the time my dad was twenty-seven, he had three kids! Of course, before I have children, I'll have to find a wife!

I do presently have a girlfriend and we enjoy each other a lot. But although I hope to be married sometime, I'm not in a hurry to make that decision right now. I have to concentrate on school, and then on getting established financially.

People sometimes ask whether I can become a father. Although it's not clear if that is medically possible for me, I like kids and hope to have a family in the future, either naturally or by adoption.

Along a similar line, people wonder if I would ever let a child of mine ride a motorcycle. I think I would, but not without a lot of instructions:

1. Always wear a helmet.
2. Enjoy riding without being a daredevil.
3. Be alert because drivers of cars often fail to see oncoming motorcycles.
4. Don't speed.

I still like to get on a cycle. I'm fixing one up at home that I can run around the farm. But I won't be doing wheelies or finding out how fast it goes. I've learned bikers don't have to take risks and ride crazily to have fun on a cycle.

A Word to Able-Bodied People

Treat a person in a wheelchair the same way you would treat any other friend.

The most thoughtful thing you can do is also the easiest—*ask* if you can help—the same as you would if you weren't sure if an able-bodied friend needed help.

People who *ask* give me dignity, so that I'm not insulted because they assume I can't do something I *am* capable of, or figure I am able to handle something that I *can't* do.

Be alert to the presence of steps, curbs, narrow doorways, and things that are out of reach for someone who is sitting. One step may prevent a person in a wheelchair from getting into a building. A new structure may be slightly cheaper if its doorways are narrow, but a wheelchair-bound person will be eliminated from it. Curb cuts and ramps allow someone like me added independence. And if counters in a bank or store are at a level I can reach, I'm saved some humiliation.

It's not only buildings that can be made more accessible, but many jobs can be, as well. Most able-bodied persons simply never consider how, with some adaptation, a disabled person could be employed by their organization. Most office jobs, many professional slots, and lots of sales and management positions can be capably filled by trained paraplegics and some quadriplegics. Insensitive employers and inaccessible buildings may be their greatest deterrent. People with spinal cord injuries have fully operational minds.

I don't mind talking about my accident and how I worked through the frustrations of my disability. Of course we don't all have the same personalities, even though we have had similar injuries, but people need not tiptoe around us, worried that we'll explode because we're carrying a bundle of anger.

You will likely hurt most of us less by asking directly about our situation, than by avoiding us, or checking with our friends about what happened, or acting as though you hadn't noticed that our legs don't work. We are human beings who enjoy giving and receiving genuine kindness and friendship. If you feel awkward, say so. If you don't know whether to open the door for me or not, ask me.

I am only as handicapped as I let myself be. Don't give me an additional handicap by limiting me in what I can do. Instead, help me to find ways to accomplish my goals and dreams.

If able-bodied people begin to be sensitive to these things, we will have better accessibility to all areas of life without our needing to fight for it. Then we can use our energies to accomplish our possibilities. Sensitivity and good communication give us the chance for independence and dignity.

We're All Handicapped

It was during my time in rehab that it first struck me—we are all handicapped in one way or another. I discovered my friends were also struggling with things that either discouraged them or stymied them in some way. I call those difficulties handicaps.

When you see me, you see my handicap. An able-bodied person's simply doesn't show as quickly. My limitation is only more obvious, but we all have hurdles to mount. Learning to handle myself physically after the accident was difficult. But my temptation to despair was an even greater struggle for me.

One month after I was hurt my Grandpa Zook died. That was a really sad time. About a month after that, I was able to take my first weekend leave from Elizabethtown. I looked forward to going home, but it turned out to be a terrible couple of days. I saw my brothers moving around, doing everything they wanted to, and I couldn't.

We did resurrect one happy tradition—Myron Stoltzfus, Jon Kent Witmer, and I had breakfast together Saturday morning. It was the first time we had done that since my accident, although we didn't follow it with a game of golf, as we usually had before.

Sunday afternoon as I was getting ready to go back to E-town, Jon Kent was killed flying his gyrocopter. I felt like the bottom was falling out of my world. I got an extension on my weekend away from the Rehab Center so I could visit Jon Kent's parents. It wasn't that I had much to say to them, but I wanted to be with them in case I could be any comfort.

My shaky faith in God began to be restored when I experienced sincere friendship from people, felt their encouragement, and recognized that they, too, were working at hardships. I saw clearly, then, that Christianity without people would be nothing.

If each of us acknowledges our own disability, it is less likely that a wall can grow between us. Then no one can feel superior to anyone else. And if we each see ourselves as somewhat needy, we may be more inclined to help each other. That's been my experience, and that's at the heart of my Christian faith.

I have a certain advantage because my handicap is so obvious. People talk to me more easily, it seems, since they know I've met with some trouble. A woman in Alberta told me this summer about how hard she's fighting depression. Her husband died, she was in a bad accident and the images of that haunt her kids every time they climb into a car. And although she's survived without physical damages, her outlook is so scarred she can barely cope. But she said that what I was doing on the road made her want to get back to living. Apparently I inspired her, but her acknowledgement kept me going, too.

A prophet's voice in the Old Testament book of Deuteronomy speaks wisdom for me: "Choose life," he says. People all across this continent encouraged me to do that on my summer journey, and I want to do the same for others. Obviously, our goals need to be set within the limits of what we can do. It would be nearly impossible for a quadriplegic to cross the country in a wheelchair because of lacking the finger control to grip the push rails. So I don't want to choose impossible tasks, but I can decide to keep going when things are hard, to keep talking with people when I don't feel like it, to slug away at whatever threatens to wear me down.

I am choosing to live. Christianity is a way of life for me, and hopefully a way I've encouraged others to go in during this summer. Naturally, I'm not perfect. The road crew can testify to that! But it is a lifestyle for me of encouragement and support to people everywhere.